Mom & Dad
Merry Christmas 1992
love Nakole

W9-AYI-567

THE GARDENER'S COMPANION

THE GARDENER'S COMPANION

SARA GODWIN

© Charles Mann

SMITHMARK

A FRIEDMAN GROUP BOOK

This edition published in 1991
by SMITHMARK Publishers Inc.
112 Madison Avenue
New York, New York 10016

Copyright © 1991 by Michael Friedman Publishing Group, Inc.

All rights reserved. No part of this publication may be reproduced,
stored in a retrieval system, or transmitted, in any form or by any
means, electronic, photocopying, recording, or otherwise, without
prior written permission of the publisher.

ISBN 0-8317-3766-2

American Garden Association
THE GARDENER'S COMPANION
was prepared and produced by
Michael Friedman Publishing Group, Inc.
15 West 26th Street
New York, NY 10010

Editors: Sharon Kalman and Robert Hernandez
Art Director: Jeff Batzli
Designer: Kevin Ullrich
Photography Editor: Christopher C. Bain

Typeset by M&D Typographers, Inc.
Color separation by Excel Graphic Arts Ltd.
Printed and bound in Hong Kong by Leefung-Asco Printers Ltd.

SMITHMARK Books are available for bulk purchase for sales
promotions and premium use. For details write or telephone the
Manager of Special Sales, SMITHMARK Publishers Inc.,
112 Madison Avenue, New York, New York 10016. (212) 532-6600.

American Garden Association is the service mark of the American
Garden Association.

DEDICATION

T o C.J., who has wandered through dozens of the world's great gardens, traipsed through hundreds of nurseries, and tromped through forests and jungles to look at flowers with me; to C.J., who has heard my theories a thousand times and is always willing to listen again; to C.J., who believes that attempting the creation of the small paradise called a garden is a worthy endeavor and who in so believing, gave me room to bloom.

ACKNOWLEDGMENTS

A ll books are the compilation of other people's knowledge, observation, and insight filtered through one's own beliefs and experience. There have been so many who shared what they knew of botany, horticulture, and dirt-under-the-nails gardening with me that I hardly know where to begin to thank them all. Paul Keiter of Gold Grade Nursery in San Rafael, California, has given me the benefit of his lifetime of experience with annuals by answering my pesky questions, albeit grumpily, for more than twenty years; Walter Doty, undoubtedly the most knowledgeable gardener I have ever met or am likely to meet, taught me that the most important thing in gardening is knowing who to ask and how to listen; and Ray Fosberg, Botanist Emeritus at the Smithsonian Institution, allowed me to tag along on scouting field trips for his tropical terrestrial botany classes in St. Croix, U.S.V.I., so many years ago, has hiked his native California hills with me patiently teaching the rudiments of botany and taxonomy, has identified numbers of plants for me, and has given me access to people and gardens all over the world. To these three, and to all the gardeners who, wherever I have wandered, have made gardening common ground and told me what grew well for them, what didn't, and why, I give my deepest appreciation and grateful thanks. All errors, God forbid, are exclusively my own.

CONTENTS

INTRODUCTION
8

Chapter One
THE PASSION
FOR GARDENING
10

Chapter Two
GARDENING TRADITIONS
26

Chapter Three
WHAT TO DO
WITH WHAT YOU'VE GOT
48

Chapter Four
THE URBANE
URBAN VINE
64

Chapter Five
THE NEGLECTABLE
GARDEN
88

Chapter Six
THE COTTAGE GARDEN
106

Chapter Seven
THE MEADOW GARDEN
126

Chapter Eight
THE LITTLE GARDEN
146

Chapter Nine
THE IMPASSIONED
GARDENER
166

SOURCES
177

BIBLIOGRAPHY
186

INDEX
188

INTRODUCTION

© Charles Mann

THIS BOOK IS A SUBVERSIVE DOCUMENT. Its purpose is to bring about a revolution in gardening by redefining and redesigning the American residential landscape. It advocates gardening as a pleasure rather than a chore, which is in itself a revolutionary notion. It advocates the pursuit of privacy in the garden, which may be socially subversive. And it advocates the abolition of the scraggly suburban lawn, which is by itself sufficient to have me banished from the land by those who believe that lawns, however wretched and weed-ridden, are sacred to the residential landscape.

I believe that gardening is a joy, richly fulfilling and deeply satisfying. I believe that most gardens could be a great deal prettier than they are with substantially less work than they currently require. I believe that gardening puts one in tune with the seasons.

Those who cherish living things learn to nurture them. Since pleasure and peace are both found in gardens, perhaps someday it will be illegal not to garden. It is in promoting a vision of a world with gardens of pleasure and peace that this book is most subversive.

CHAPTER ONE

THE PASSION FOR GARDENING

WHY ON EARTH DOES ANYONE GARDEN? IT is a lifetime of work building a place of loveliness out of plants. It is never the same from year to year, month to month, day to day, or even moment to moment, for a garden is an exacting study in constant change. Certainly it is a clear demonstration of human limitation, for the gardener controls none of the essential elements—not the shining of the sun or the falling of the rain or the changing of the seasons or even what grows on this small piece of the planet—as every weed declares and demonstrates.

It is not easy to build a garden. Ask any gardener straightening a creaking back bent from setting seedlings or pulling weeds. Ask any gardener who has raised a blister digging holes in recalcitrant soil. Ask

Rhododendrons celebrate spring with a flourish. They grow best in acid soil and filtered light.

any gardener who has spent long hours puzzling out a planting scheme of what will grow where and what will bloom when.

Yet gardeners continue to garden. For every complaint, there is a compensating joy. One day, the tree shades, the flowers bloom. Not the day they are planted, perhaps, but *one* day, making a gardener's life one of delicious anticipation of a hope-filled future.

A garden teaches what it is to be human, for every possible emotion may be elicited there. There is the joy of bringing a difficult plant to bloom, like the burgundy lady-slipper orchid (*Paphiopedilum*) that is blooming in the conservatory for the first time in the fifteen years I've owned it. There is the incandescent rage whenever the deer breach the ramparts and browse the roses to pitiful mutilated stubs. There is the "little quiet peace" of walking through the garden in the morning with a cup of tea to see what's come up or budded or bloomed.

For those who garden—and their numbers are legion, nearly eighty million households in the United States alone—there is no need to explain or explicate why one gardens. Those who garden already know the pleasurable temptation inherent in a plot of freshly turned earth. And no plot is more insidious, for it would cheerfully demand every waking moment to rake it smooth, broadcast seeds, set out seedlings, mulch or weed, water and fertilize, until there are flowers for the house or vegetables for the table.

No, the explanations must be made to those who cannot feel the pull of the earth, who are not tugged outdoors by the first breath of spring, who do not count the days until the seeds arrive, the soil thaws, the seedlings come up, the trees leaf out, the first buds appear, the flowers bloom, and the fruit ripens. They will never know the agony of the gardener when the wind knocks down the delphiniums, the hail batters the corn, the sun will not shine, or the rains do not come. They are baffled by the utter absorption of the gardener at a rhododendron nursery or a daffodil society show. My daughter's roommate is among these. Jane's houseplants—including trees stretching up ten feet tall—flourish in her Victorian flat in lavish profusion; her roommate mutters of acquiring a machete in order to hack her way to the door in case of an emergency that would require a hasty exit.

Gardening demonstrates more clearly than any other activity I know that the things we want to do are fun and the things someone else wants us to do are work. If someone ordered us to get up early on the weekend and slave from dawn to dusk up to our elbows in mud, we could probably get any court in the land to overturn the sentence as cruel and unusual punishment. Yet gardeners will daydream away hours planning a weekend doing precisely that. Many's the suburban soul who'd sooner sneak off fishing than mow the lawn, yet those confined to city apartments pray for the day when they can buy a place in the country with an old orchard to prune, acres of rocks to transform into meadows of flowers, and a cottage to cover with roses and morning-glories.

It is said that the Creator began with a garden, and it seems only proper and fitting that we, created in that image, should do no less.

THE PRIVILEGE OF PEACE AND PRIVACY

When I was still a child it occurred to me that I might never be very rich. I wondered what it was the rich spent their money on, that they needed so much of it. I learned by observation—not, alas, experience—that the rich *don't* spend their money, which is how they became and remain very rich. Instead of spending, the rich invest. That means that whatever they spend on ends up being worth more when they're done, which makes them even richer. From my observation, the things that the rich invest the most in are sunshine, quiet, and privacy.

I cannot tell you how to become rich, but I can tell you how to achieve sunshine, quiet, and privacy in your garden. And if one can have what the rich spend their money on without the family fortune, why, that will do. As the French say, enough is as good as a feast.

The Venerable Hedge

Nothing could be less conducive to privacy than most urban and suburban landscaping. The cliché of a lawn, shrubs at the base of the house, and a lonely tree or two pretty well characterizes the residential landscape. In most cities, the difference between urban and suburban can be observed in a glance by the size of the lawn. The more urban the setting, the smaller the lawn until, in the most urban settings, it disappears entirely.

To achieve privacy there must be a visual barrier between public areas and private areas, between the street or sidewalk and the house. Most people achieve privacy by hanging curtains or drapes, and zap! there goes the sunshine. A hedge, on the other hand, is attractive to look at, makes curtains and drapes unnecessary, absorbs noise and dust, and makes an excellent background for a pretty flower border, thus improving the view from those same windows that, once rid of their curtains, drapes, louvers, shades, and other "window treatments," will flood the house with sunshine and light. To achieve all these wondrous things Americans must abandon their habit of little bitty hedges. Two-foot, three-foot, four-foot hedges don't make the cut. Privacy hedges must be at least six feet high, preferably higher. Tall hedges create the feeling of a medieval walled garden, where the noise and haste of the outside world are left where they belong: outside.

Besides providing privacy from both the casual passerby and the inquisitive neighbor, hedges have another splendid advantage: They block out unattractive views, whether it is a neighboring house built too close for comfort, the children's play area in the backyard, or the neon signs of nearby commercial establishments. Hedges also work as windbreaks, creating a small island of sheltered stillness in the garden, as the wind passes harmlessly over the tall hedges and the house.

Any number of plants work well as hedges. The English tradition is to trim trees into tall hedges, ten feet high and more, and four to six feet wide. They often use yew (*Taxus*), hornbeam (*Carpinus*), beech (*Fagus*), and hawthorn (*Crataegus*). Americans tend to grow lower, narrower hedges using boxwood (*Buxus* spp.), privet (*Ligustrum*), firethorn (*Pyracantha*), cotoneaster (*Cotoneaster*), holly (*Ilex* spp.), or English laurel (*Prunus laurocerasus*). Tall bamboos make excellent, graceful hedges, but be sure to use clumping bamboos rather than run-

Bamboo makes an excellent privacy hedge—tall enough to screen, dense enough to absorb noise and dust, and ever so much prettier than a fence.

ning bamboos or they'll spread all over creation and beyond. Clumping bamboos include *Bambusa*, *Chusquea*, *Otatea*, *Sinarundinaria*, and *Thamnocalamus*; most are tropical or subtropical. Running bamboos include *Arundinaria*, *Chimonobambusa*, *Phyllostachys*, *Pseudosasa*, *Sasa*, *Semiarundinaria*, and *Shibataea*, and most are fairly hardy, being native to temperate zones of China and Japan.

Good hedging bamboos are *Bambusa glaucescens*: *B.g.* 'Alphonse Karr', yellow stems brilliantly striped with green; *B.g.* 'Fernleaf', which looks best grown in poor soil with minimal water, since in rich soil with plenty of water, the leaf shape changes and becomes coarse; *B.g.* 'Golden Goddess'; and *B.g.*

rivierorum, the Chinese Goddess bamboo, with tiny leaves in lacy fernlike sprays. All of these bamboos will tolerate temperatures down to fifteen degrees F, except the species proper, which becomes unbecomingly crisp below twenty degrees F. In warm climates, escallonia, oleander, and hibiscus make fine flowering hedges.

There are any number of other plants that can be persuaded to make hedges. In Kauai, Vanda orchids are used as a low hedge. In St. Croix, U.S.V.I., I saw a pencil tree (*Euphorbia tirucalli*) grown into an impenetrable thirty-foot hedge that the owner referred to as her "security system." Its branches

are brittle and bleed profusely when broken; the sap is poisonous and locally rumored to cause blindness if it gets in the eyes. Burglars would rather go nose-to-nose with a pair of rottweilers than breach her hedge. I designed a bright bougainvillea bramble to accomplish the same end for a house at Los Cabos in Baja California—bougainvillea's thorns are more than adequate to give prowlers second thoughts. In colder climates, holly or hawthorn can serve the same purpose, if you consider security to be part of privacy.

Hedges, now that I think about it, have an undeservedly bad reputation on both ends. They

A bougainvillea hedge offers security as well as privacy—it has vicious thorns to go with its beautiful and brilliant bracts.

Holly branches make classic Christmas greens and the bright red berries provide important winter provender for birds.

are popularly believed to take a long time to grow, and, once grown, to require a lot of work to trim. Neither is true. It seems unfair, somehow, that hedges should stand accused first of not growing fast enough, and then, of growing too fast.

I am a bit of a heretic on the subject of trimming; hedges manicured weekly to rigid right angles put me off. Think of your hedge as thick and lush rather than shaggy, and one or two trims a year will probably be plenty.

How long a hedge takes to fill in depends on what you plant, on your soil, water, and climate, on all the variables, in fact, that make writing a gardening book for worldwide distribution such a headache because no statement can be made without a flurry of qualifiers and exceptions. But

no matter what hedging material you choose or the climate you live in, you can have a handsome hedge and genuine privacy in five years or less.

When choosing a hedge, remember that it is an investment. You are not merely gardening recreationally. You are increasing the value of the property. Plant as thickly as your checkbook allows. (Perhaps the neighbors will split the cost with you since they will also enjoy the benefit.) Dig deeply—at least twelve inches deeper than the root ball—toss in a slow-release fertilizer, and water well.

To trim a hedge, make it slightly narrower at the top than at the base to allow light to reach the lower leaves; otherwise, hedges get thin and leggy at the bottom.

To renovate a sparse hedge, whack off between one-third and one-half of its height in early spring. If you can't bring yourself to be so brutal, plant a flower border in front of it with tall flowers in the rear, the hedge as a background. While the observer's eye is distracted by the pretty border, whack away with a will to force new growth at the bottom so the hedge can return to its proper glory. (Some hedges are best trimmed by removing whole branches from the bottom; ask a knowledgeable nurseryperson and show them a small branch so they know what you have.)

Holly, cotoneaster, and firethorn all have bright winter berries, and you can do most of an annual trim cutting greens for the house at Christmas. Privet also has berries, as do the other three hedges; they attract songbirds to the garden. Hibiscus and escallonia attract hummingbirds. Hawthorn can get its yearly haircut in the spring when you bring in budded branches to force for

Firethorn is a good year-round hedge with flowers in spring and red berries in winter, while the grapevine makes a fine summer screen, offering handsome leaves, summer fruit, and autumn color.

17

large bouquets. (The English name for hawthorn is Maythorn because it is believed to bloom on May Day. The "haw" is the berry, the thorn, self-explanatory.) Yew and oleander are both poisonous, something to keep in mind if you keep livestock or have children around who are at that age when anything that fits in their mouth is considered edible. Yew is also a fast-growing evergreen, dense, tolerant of wind and cold, with the charming ability to make the most modest home appear to be an English countryseat.

Hedges need not be used only to border the property lines. They are also a good way to screen areas of the yard that are useful but not exactly scenic. For example, the children's play yard with its swing set and sandbox, a dog run, the garage or storage shed, the trash cans, or a back alley. Even the cutting garden or vegetable plot can be tucked neatly out of sight behind a hedge.

A Little Quiet Peace

Because foliage absorbs sound more effectively than do solid surfaces like walls and fences, hedges contribute substantially to quiet. While foliage dampens sound, splashing water masks it. Remember all those spy movies where the good guy turns on the faucet in the bathroom and lets it run so the bad guys listening through the wall can't hear what he's saying? Well, the trick works just as well outdoors. If you have a year-round brook on the property, cherish it. If not, a fountain, however small, will accomplish the same end: the soothing, pleasing sound of falling water.

The burble, bubble, tinkle, and trickle of splashing water helps drown out the noise of neighbors and traffic.

Pools are the place to grow lovely waterlilies like these as well as other water-loving plants.

A garden fountain makes it possible to see a rainbow any sunny day, and the smooth water of the pool creates an everchanging play of light that sparkles and shines across its surface. Recirculating pumps conserve water.

A quiet, sunny corner of the garden is a perfect place for breakfast or to sit and contemplate the trees and flowers.

Fountains need not be either extravagant or wasteful of water. Recirculating pumps allow the same water to be used over and over. A pretty fountain can consist of no more than a tall stone urn drilled through the bottom to provide space for a water pipe, placed on a pile of large rocks. The water fills the urn, spills over the sides, and splashes down the rocks into a little pool, where it is pumped back into the urn. Small wall fountains make it possible to enjoy the sound of splashing water in the smallest garden, even if it is little more than an air shaft in the middle of a city.

Trees help dispel noise, too, as sound is carried up and over the tops. Within the walls of the garden the sight of passing traffic is banished, and its sound as well.

A Place in the Sun

But what of sunshine, you ask? Only trim your trees for filtered light, allowing the sun to dapple the grass with a chiaroscuro of sunlight and shadow. Leave open spaces where the sun can shine onto a stone terrace, where a table may be set for breakfast on a bright morning. Trim foundation plants that have grown too high away from the windows. Let the house be filled with light.

To me, one of life's tragedies is spending a beautiful day indoors. I think people should go to work on rainy days when they have a cold and call in sick on beautiful days, to revel in the sun, having already given work its due.

REDEFINING THE LANDSCAPE

I propose nothing less than to redefine and redesign the residential landscape. I see the garden as a refuge from a hurried, harried world, a world best left behind when the garden gate swings closed. Whether the garden itself is a riot of bright color within its walls, or a peaceful palette of green, it should be a place where one may sit in quiet contemplation of the ways of the world or watch laughing children play.

There is more, of course. The redefinition of the American landscape has already begun with the desire to preserve what wilderness still remains, whether it is centuries-old forest or sweeping prairie. It is present in the new wave of landscape fashions that include the meadow garden, the woodland garden, the native plant garden, and the wildflower garden. It is present in the introduction of the hedgerow to American roadsides, similar to those that characterize the English countryside. One English gardening book that recently appeared proposed the planting of what was charmingly described as a "tapestry hedge." It consists of holly, hawthorn, field maple (*Acer campestre*), buckthorn (*Rhamnus*), sallow (*Salix caprea*), cotoneaster, privet, pyracantha, and *Rosa rugosa*. It has flowers, berries, and fall color, everything one could possibly hope for from a hedge. Be forewarned: The more rampant species will eventually smother the less vigorous plants, but judicious pruning should keep it attractive for many years. In the meantime, it forms a living tapestry of birds, bright berries, and flowers.

The tapestry hedge is not terribly dissimilar from the English hedgerow. Originally planted to divide fields and keep sheep off the roads, English hedgerows have ended up screening houses and pastures alike from the inevitable noise and dirt of traffic. I am seeing a similar development where I live in northern California. Some years ago I was on a tree committee that persuaded the town to plant the bare slopes of a raised-railroad-track-turned-surface-road with a double row of trees. The raised roadbed is bordered by frontage roads on either side lined with modest houses. As the

Gray squirrels like this one often assist me with the landscaping: they dig up the bulbs, discover they aren't nuts, and courteously replant them—usually somewhere else, making the garden full of spring surprises.

trees grew up and transformed the raised road into a pretty avenue, the people who lived along the frontage roads planted shrubs and flowers between the trees, which had already begun to screen the houses off entirely from the passing cars. The homeowners gain privacy, the motorist gains a prettier drive, and the entire town benefits.

In addition, hedgerows provide food and cover for birds and those small creatures referred to as "urban wildlife" that are timidly creeping back to live in concert with people. It is a pretty way to help restore the ecological balance of a land once so rich with wildlife that the early explorers doubted that anyone back home would believe their reports of the vast abundance.

The return of urban and suburban wildlife is important, too. The wild creatures that frequent my garden include gray squirrels, possum, dusky-footed wood rats, alligator lizards, raccoons, black-tail deer, and the occasional passing skunk. The woods that surround my house are home to great horned owls, fox, and bobcats as well, but I only get the briefest glimpses of them every now and then. There are probably forty or more species of birds that either live here year-round or drop by on their journey along the Pacific Flyway, a sort of highway of the sky. Red-tailed hawks, turkey vultures, and little screech owls share the wooded hillside with yellow warblers, Bewick's wrens, hermit thrushes, rufous-sided towhees, brown towhees, varied thrushes, kinglets, bushtits, tit-mice, song sparrows, dark-eyed juncos, brown creepers, purple finches, house finches, chestnut-backed chickadees, orange-shafted flickers, scrub jays, and the handsomely crested bright blue Steller's jays. Anna's hummingbirds are year-round residents and both Allen's and Rufous hummingbirds stop off to rest on their way north in the spring, and sometimes on their way south

*In my heart of hearts I believe that deer are large rodents: The only things in the garden I know for certain they will **not** eat are rhododendrons, oleander, and Sonoma fieldstone.*

at the end of summer as well. The Western tanagers, black-headed grosbeaks, and cedar waxwings show up when the hawthorn, the cherries, or the figs are ripe.

Seed feeders and hummingbird feeders supplement the food the birds find in the garden. More important to me, the feeders are hung just outside the windows where I can get a close-up view. It never fails to astonish me how fearless birds are if one sits quietly in their midst. I've had bushtits walk right over my shoes, pecking industriously, and hummingbirds hover inches from my face, no less interested in me than I in them.

There has been another curious development since we began feeding the birds. Tent caterpillars used to strip the trees until we felt compelled to spray to save the oaks. Last year there weren't enough tents to bother spraying, and this year

The raccoons only come at night, bringing their little ones to drink and wash at the birdbath.

we've had none at all. Several years ago the oak moths swarmed in such profusion it was impossible to sit outside. We bought one of those dreadful "bug zappers" and cringed as it fried moths all night long. Since we hung a collection of bird feeders, in the last few years, we've had no moths at all. The yellow jacket wasps used to render eating outdoors in the summer to an exercise in frantic arm flapping; we found eleven nests on the property one year. This year we found one. The tree mosquitoes used to leave me a mass of bites every time I gardened in any clothing providing less coverage than a bedouin burnoose. This year we hung seven hummingbird feeders, and the mosquitos have pretty much vanished. I know that hummingbirds eat huge numbers of insects, and I'm sure that some of the little birds I can't identify are flycatchers, but there seems to be a direct correlation between the phenomenon of more birds of more different kinds in the garden, and far fewer insects. Is this what the balance of nature is all about? I think so.

The Definition of Paradise

With sunshine, quiet, and privacy, a pervasive calm steals over the garden. Songbirds nest in the trees, splash and drink at the fountain, feed on the insects and berries, and welcome each morning with song. Hummingbirds sip nectar from the flowers. Butterflies dance on the air, and peace descends. Paradise may mean no more than "garden," but that's enough.

The purpose of a garden is to provide pleasure and peace. Planting easy, hardy perennials like these daylilies leaves more time for the contemplation of beauty, which is one of the greatest pleasures of having a garden.

CHAPTER TWO

GARDENING TRADITIONS

A MERICAN GARDENING TRADITIONS HAVE as much to do with Europe as they do with America. The English colonists brought one set of gardening traditions with them, and the Spanish *padres* another. The English set up greens and commons for grazing sheep and planted kitchen gardens. The Spanish missionaries brought the Mediterranean traditions of deep adobe-tiled verandas looking out on thick-walled courtyards planted with citrus and figs, and outside the courtyard walls, vineyards and olive groves. Where each settled, their stamp remains.

At the same time, the Old World was eagerly planting the trees and flowers brought back from the New World in its gardens and glasshouses. One of Capt. James Cook's commissions was to bring back plants

The Palm House at Kew Gardens, London, is the finest surviving example of Victorian conservatory architecture.
Some of the trees there are hundreds of years old, brought back from the South Seas by Captain Cook.

from his voyages of exploration, which took him from England to Australia, New Zealand, and Tasmania, through the islands of the South Pacific, across the Pacific to the west coast of North America, along the coasts of South America, across the Atlantic to Africa and up the west coast of Africa and Europe back to England. Captain Bligh, immortalized in *Mutiny on the Bounty*, was dispatched to Tahiti to collect breadfruit to be planted in the West Indies to provide food for the slaves on the Caribbean sugar plantations so their owners need not be put to the expense of feeding them.

The terrarium, originally called the Wardian case, was invented by Dr. Nathaniel Ward as a method of bringing seedlings back alive from these long ocean voyages, which often lasted several years. The artificial environment of a glass case kept alive seedlings and slips that otherwise could not have survived the drying winds and the salt spray of homeward-bound voyages that often took years before the ship sailed back into her home port. There is a tree brought back by Captain Cook nearly three hundred years ago that lives today in the palm house at Kew Gardens in London, perhaps the world's leading botanical garden. Other collections are found in the Physic Garden not far from Sloane Square in London with which Nathaniel Ward was closely connected.

ENGLISH GARDENING TRADITIONS

It is the gardening traditions of England that have influenced the American residential landscape most heavily. From that damp, green island where rainfall is so certain that the broad greenswards of the Royal Botanic Garden at Kew have no sprink-

lers, America got the most backbreaking burden of suburban gardening, the ubiquitous lawn.

England gave America more than the yearning for broad, rolling lawns. England also gave it the benefit of her long tradition of water in the garden, of streams, canals, lakes, ponds, cascades, and pretty little brooks. This particular gift came largely from Lancelot "Capability" Brown (1715-1783), the leading landscape architect of the mid-eighteenth century. His nickname derived from his assurance to those of the nobility and gentry who could afford his services that their vast parklands had "capability"; just as landscape architects and interior decorators today assure their clients that their places have "potential."

Cherry trees in bloom on the mossy banks of a dry stream make an enchanting alternative to a backyard lawn.

Natural Landscapes

Prior to the advent of Mr. Brown, England's country estates had drawn heavily on the formal French tradition. To create the natural landscapes with rivers and woodlands he believed were more truly English, Capability improved the formal gardens derived from the French until they were virtually nonexistent, bidding "*adieu* to canals, circular basins, and cascades tumbling down marble steps, the last absurd magnificence of Italian and French villas," in the words of Horace Walpole in *An Essay on Modern Gardening* (1785). (Actually, the comment was made about William Kent, but it is no less true of Capability Brown.) Between 1749 and 1783 Brown landscaped one hundred of England's greatest gardens, including Blenheim Palace, Oxfordshire; Leeds Castle, Kent; Longleat, Wiltshire; Warwick Castle, Warwickshire; and Sheffield Park, Sussex. The only seventeenth-century garden in England not leveled by Brown's naturalism is Melbourne Hall, Derbyshire, built in 1696 by Henry Wise.

Grape hyacinths (Muscari armeniacum) *are one of those lovely plants that cooperate with the gardener by making a natural landscape.*

The Cottage Garden

From England came the cottage garden, that happy combination of flowers, herbs, and vegetables in one delightful dooryard bouquet. The herbaceous border is also in the great English gardening tradition, perfected by Gertrude Jekyll (1843–1932) at the turn of the century. Many of the flowers she chose to use in her borders were from the cottage gardens of an earlier era. Jekyll was a professional painter, a contemporary of the French Impressionists, and when her eyesight began to fail her in her fifties she turned to gardening, creating painterly effects in the herbaceous borders for which she is famous. The herbaceous border at her home at Munstead Wood, Surrey, was two hundred feet long by eighteen feet wide, and was backed by shrubs against a sandstone wall covered with climbers. She wrote regularly for William Robinson's *Gardening Illustrated*, but she did not publish her first book, *Wood and Garden* (1899), until she was fifty-six.

From William Robinson (1838–1944), whose book *The English Flower Garden* is one of the seminal works of gardening, came the happy habit of naturalizing lovely things like great drifts of daffodils and banks of primroses, finding what would grow well and reseed itself.

The Victorians contributed carpet bedding, the planting of large flower beds to a single species of a single color, like the endless bed of red tulips seen every spring in St. James Park, London. Carpet bedding is now, for the most part, primarily a practice of those who landscape public parks and those who spell out the names of large corporations in sempervivum or dwarf boxwood on the slopes above subsurface freeways.

The Rock Garden

The English are inveterate travelers and equally inveterate plant collectors and these two passions combined in the rock garden, which also has its adherents in the United States. Tiny alpine plants with even tinier flowers are tucked into niches and pockets between boulders that have been piled to look as much like Alpine outcroppings and scree as the imitative arts can manage. Reginald Farrer was the father of the rock garden, and when the first public rock garden was nearly ready for display, he was invited to the Royal Botanic Garden at Edinburgh, Scotland, to view it. An imperious and irascible sort, Farrer told them they'd done it all wrong and it ought to be done over entirely. And it was. His classic book, *The English Rock Garden* (2 vols., 1919), is still valuable, still violently opinionated (plants he didn't like are described as "insipid"), and great fun to read.

This rock garden has flowers tucked in around the rocks and steps and a little waterfall to splash over the rocks in the stream.

The Spanish traditions of architecture and gardening cope beautifully with heat and drought. Thick adobe walls keep interiors cool and drought-resistant plants like bougainvillea, salvia, and cacti flourish with relatively little water.

THE SPANISH GARDEN TRADITION

The traditions the Spanish friars and settlers of the great Spanish land grants brought with them to the New World were essentially Mediterranean, with a *soupçon* of Moorish influence tossed in. The missions had adobe-walled courtyards, paved and often tiled, with a cool fountain bubbling in the center. Vines grew up the walls and huge clay pots held citrus trees. Medicinal and culinary herbs were often cultivated within the walls. Flowers were almost incidental. Vast vineyards and olive groves surrounded the missions' walls.

The great Spanish *haciendas* had walls as much as four feet thick, red tiled roofs, glazed tile floors, and long, low-shadowed verandas. Thick walls kept the house cool during the day and warm at night. Herbs, vegetables, and flowers were all grown separately, as were crops. Huge paved courtyards marked the entrance to the house. Both the courtyards and the shady verandas were decorated with potted plants, and vines twined up the posts of the veranda. A tree or two might shade the courtyard and the *hacienda* from the midday sun. In this dry new land the emphasis was heavily practical: Whatever used precious water had to produce. Edible plants received far more attention than ornamentals, and the Spanish introduced the Old World's grape, citrus and olive trees to the New World. Orchards of fruit trees, sometimes protected by rows of taller trees used for windbreaks, were more commonly planted than trees that merely shaded or looked pretty.

Today the Spanish tradition has been greatly modified. The courtyard has become the backyard patio, the great barbecues that roasted whole steers have become the barbecue grills sizzling on the backyard patio, the vineyards for sacramental wines have become the California wine industry, and the long, low lines of the *haciendas* have been translated into the single-story, ranch-style house beloved by suburban developers across the nation.

Spanish- or Mediterranean-style stucco houses, common throughout Southern California, still look best whitewashed and covered with clambering bougainvillea. Most would probably look better without the scrap of lawn in front, substituting instead the walled courtyard that gives a bit of privacy even in those cities where houses are built in close proximity to one another.

The English traditions of landscaping began on the East Coast and marched steadily westward with the pioneers. The Spanish, having come primarily for gold and conquest rather than settlement, wandered about more, from Florida into Mexico and up from Mexico into Texas, the

A water-conservative garden (above) *need not look either sparse or parched, as this garden at the Carmel Mission in Carmel, California, clearly demonstrates. The flowers are* Pelargonium peltatum *and* Salvia leucantha.

Lushly planted interior courtyards like this one (left) *in Florida, complete with the soft splashing of a fountain, are a pleasant refuge from the harried, work-a-day world.*

The California pepper tree (Schinus molle) *casts a graceful shade, and has delicate, shell-pink fruits as well.*

whole Southwest, and California as far north as Sacramento. The Spanish tradition was adapted to subtropical plants in southern Florida with huge-leaved philodendrons scaling walls and filling courtyards with lush greenery, to the deserts of Texas and the Southwest with cacti creating sculptural silhouettes against white walls, and to the temperate climates where California pepper trees (*Schinus molle*), shaded patios, and lemon and orange trees (*Citrus* spp.) are hung with bright fruit and fragrant blossoms even in the midst of winter.

The Two Traditions

In some ways the Spanish tradition is more urban in its origins, the English tradition, more pastoral. The English tradition looks best with great sweeps of land, endless acres of lawn fading into meadow,

Not all of the color in courtyards built in the Spanish tradition comes from the flowers: Some comes from the patterned ceramic tile on the steps.

© Charles Mann

A walled courtyard is a good alternative to a lawn in hot, dry climates. Hollyhocks set off the gate to this garden in New Mexico.

woodland segueing into forest, stream flowing into river or lake. The Spanish tradition, with its verandas, patios, and courtyards, works better in confined spaces because it defines limits rather than providing long views to the horizon. It creates privacy with walls, not limitless expanses of land.

The English landscape tradition has been transformed over the last two or three centuries, just as the Spanish has. From immense lawns kept clipped by picturesque flocks of sheep we now have the suburban lawn kept clipped by a scowling homeowner; from one-acre kitchen gardens we now have a small plot of tomatoes and corn; from

herb gardens in elaborate and intricate shapes we now tuck some parsley and chives under the foundation plants or in a flowerpot; the woodland has become a half-dozen trees, no two alike, confined to a small backyard.

THE CALIFORNIA TRADITION

So far, the United States has produced only one clear landscaping style of its own, the California style. It made its debut in 1948 on the cover of

House Beautiful, with a garden designed by Thomas Church and Lawrence Halperin for the Dewey Donnells of Sonoma, California. It featured a free-form pool complete with a sinuous sculpture in the middle to swim under or bask on. The primary tenet of the new philosophy was that gardens are for people rather than plants. The style is characterized by wooden decks, swimming pools, terraces, play yards for children, and service areas for garages, tool sheds, trash containers, and similar essentials of urban and suburban living. Trees, shrubs, and flowers get fitted in along the edges, in planters or pots that will not interfere with the family's activities. The garden has become a place to put a picnic table, a chaise lounge, and a barbecue. It is uncluttered, functional, and easy for busy people to maintain. As it happens, I don't consider a combination of concrete, gravel, and juniper gardening. Rather it is a way to keep the neighbors off your back about the looks of the yard.

Perhaps this is the point at which I should say: America is growing up. Children think gardening is work; adults know it is a pleasure. Children call the space surrounding the house the yard; adults call it the garden. There is a difference between a yard and a garden. Yards are places to store things, as in construction yard or maintenance yard or play yard. Gardens are places to grow things, as in flowers, fruits, herbs, and a wise philosophy. Yards are about function; gardens are about beauty. It is not especially difficult to transform a yard into a garden. The hardest part is the change of attitude.

If the front lawn is inappropriate to much of American landscaping, what else might be done with that space? Given that lawns the size of a postage stamp look silly, and that unkempt lawns are guaranteed to arouse the ire of neighbors and spouses, to what better use might that land be put? In a time when privacy is practically beyond

Swimming pools require their own form of landscaping, preferably with trees too far away to drop leaves in the water and no overhanging branches. Ornamental grasses like these are a low-maintenance solution to the combination of plants and swimming pools.

The "gardens are for people" school of landscaping gives over large areas of the garden to steps, terraces, tables, patios, pathways, and other non-flowering accoutrements of landscape.

price, I would suggest walled gardens. In a world where native species are disappearing at a frightening rate, I would urge gardens that include sensitive and thoughtful collections of native plants, particularly since endemic species are already adapted to the region, making the garden far less demanding and far more rewarding for the gardener. (*A word of warning:* Too many species of native plants are endangered for collecting in the wild to be a legitimate form of acquisition. Unless you are rescuing plants doomed to death by development, unless the bulldozer is imminent, don't dig wild plants. Seeds for most wildflowers, cacti, succulents, and native ferns can be purchased from specialist nurseries.)

If the space is small, perhaps a cottage garden is best: a riotous bouquet of bright color through spring, summer, and fall, behind a pretty, open-worked wrought iron fence. A larger space might be suited to a formal *parterre* of clipped boxwood with flowers in the spaces between the geometric shapes formed by the boxwood. A walled garden with fruit trees espaliered along the inside and flowering vines climbing up and tumbling over the top is a fine way to make the world go away. A Japanese garden with a hedge of bamboo, a stepping-stone path to the door, a stone water basin gently trickling water, mosses, maples (*Acer* spp.), and azaleas (*Rhododendron* spp.) all bespeak a soft serenity. A medieval knot garden of dark green germander (*Teucrium*), silvery artemisia (*Artemisia ludoviciana*), light green dwarf boxwood (*Buxus sempervireas* 'Suffruticosa'), and lavender (*Lavandula angustifolia*) makes a striking picture, especially when the spaces of the knot are planted in summer with bright flowers. A well-tended herb garden is full of sweet smells and delicious flavors, wonderful contrasts of color and texture and flowers. Plant fennel (*Foeniculum vulgare*) near angelica (*Angelica archangelica*), dill (*Anethum graveolens*) near borage (*Borago officinalis*), cardoon

Japanese gardens are characterized by simplicity and a sense of serenity that are far more welcoming than a conventional front-yard lawn with tricycles in the driveway and roller skates on the porch.

(*Cynara cardunculus*) near rosemary (*Rosmarinus officinalis*), pineapple sage (*Salvia elegans*) near sweet bay (*Laurus nobilis*), and edge the beds all around with English lavender or curled parsley (*Petroselinum crispum*). One cannot help but see what pretty things herbs may be.

Build an arbor from the gate to the door and make it a tunnel of wisteria or old roses. Instead of dull shrubs around the foundation, plant clinging vines or espalier fruit trees along the sides of the house. (Heat lost through the walls of the house keeps vines green longer and makes fruits bear earlier.) Plant a ground cover of alpine strawberries (*Fragaria* 'Baron Solemacher') beneath the espaliers, or flowering kale (*Brassica oleracea*) mixed with red and green chard (*Beta vulgaris*). Edge a path with curled parsley and pansies (*Viola* x *Wittrockiana*) for an edible landscape.

Don't drain marshy land to plant a lawn; make a bog garden with massive-leaved Gunnera, white Siberian iris (*Iris sibirica*), gloriously scarlet Cardinal flower (*Lobelia fulgens* or *L. Cardinalis*), white meadowsweet (*Filipendula*), primrose (*Primula* spp.), lots of ferns, and huge white calla lilies (*Zantedeschia aethiopica* 'Hercules'). For trees, grow sweet gum (*Liquidambar styraciflua*), golden weeping willow (*Salix alba tristis, S. babylonica aurea* 'Niobe'), rose-gold pussy willow (*S. gracilistyla*), or Alaska blue willow (*S. purpurea*), sour gum (*Nyssa sylvatica*), or almost any of the birches (*Betula* spp.), beeches, or aspens (*Populus* spp.). If there's room left over for a discreet shrub, plant blueberries (*Vaccinium* spp.).

Any of these ideas would make for a striking front yard, certainly more personal, more individual, and more interesting than a struggling lawn. There are dozens more, but to get a sense of the structure of such a garden, consider the following woodland garden.

Wisteria blooming in fragrant profusion against a wall makes a striking entry to a house.

Flowering dogwood, with its lovely white flowers in spring and bright red foliage in fall, is a choice selection for a woodland garden.

A Woodland Garden

A strip of woodland can balance a two- or three-story house handsomely or completely hide a single-story house. Consider massing birches, small maples, cherry ((*Prunus sargenti, P. serrula, P. serrulata*), dogwood (*Cornus* spp.), red-osier dogwood (*C. stolonifera*), and golden-twig dogwood (*C.s.* 'Flaviramea').

These four species alone mark the passing of the seasons in all their wonder. Birch leaves turn brilliant yellow in the fall, the maples color red and orange and yellow, and the dogwoods, a rich, rich red. Against winter's snow paper birches have white trunks streaked up and down with gray; the

cherry has shining burgundy bark with dark stripes around the trunk; the red-osier has clear red branches that cheer equally whether silhouetted against new snow or dark skies; and the golden-twig dogwood gives the same effect as the red-osier but in yellow.

Maples, too, can be selected for the color and texture of their bark. The Sangokaku Japanese maple (*Acer palmatum* 'Sangokaku') has scarlet bark; David's maple (*A. davidii*) has green bark striped with silver; the new twigs of the Rocky Mountain maple (*A. glabrum*) are crimson, eventually turning dark so the tree is always dark in the center and red at the edge; paperbark maple (*A. griseum*) has a fascinating reddish brown bark that perpetually peels in papery pieces; and sugar maple

There are few sights as soul-satisfying as a sugar maple in full fall splendor. What a pleasure to come home to.

Here is a pretty woods, a small stream, and a simple bridge to sit and dangle one's feet from while contemplating nature's beauty.

(*A. saccharum*), which has silver-gray bark. These are but a few of the maples that are readily available. A collection of maples could easily keep the keen gardener blissfully absorbed.

In spring the birches in this little woodland have pale green leaves; the maples may have new leaves of bronze or pink or red; the dogwood, leaves of bright green. Large, open, white or pink flowers completely cover the dogwood when it blooms. The cherry creates a bower of white blossoms that are as beautiful in bouquets as they are in the woods.

In summer, the cherry has delicious, dangling red fruit, equally delightful and desirable to people, birds, and squirrels. The dogwoods have clusters of scarlet berries that last into winter or until the birds eat them. Flowers, fruit, fall color, winter drama, and wildlife, all achieved by planting only four species of trees in a space that need be no more than twenty feet square.

Every woodland must have a canopy of tall trees, an understory of smaller trees, a shrub understory, and shade-loving herbaceous plants. This woodland would look lovely with an understory of native rhododendrons, azaleas, and daphne (*Daphne odora* 'Marginata'). For pockets of carefree color, add bulbs: snowdrops (*Galanthus* spp.), giant crocus (*Colchicum*), purple *Iris reticulata*, yellow *I. danfordiae*, dwarf daffodils (*Narcissus* spp.) [try 'February Gold', 'February Silver', 'Angel's Tears', and 'Tête-à-Tête'], Poet's Narcissus (*N. poeticus* 'Actaea'), Chinese sacred lilies (*N. tazetta orientalis*), white 'Thalia' (*N.t.* 'Thalia'), and white lily-of-the-valley (*Convallaria*).

Wildflowers grow well in the filtered light of a small woodland. Ordinarily, wildflowers require less care than most garden flowers.

Daffodils are excellent for naturalizing in a woodland setting. With sufficient summer water, they spread and bloom year after year.

Bulbs make early spring especially lovely in a woodland garden as these white snowdrops and bright yellow winter aconite beautifully demonstrate.

Fill in with woodland wildflowers such as blue, white, and yellow violets (*Viola* spp.), wake-robin (*Trillium*), fawn lily (*Erythronium californicum*), shooting-star (*Dodecatheon*), Solomon's seal (*Polygonatum*), baby blue-eyes (*Nemophila menziesii*), meadowsweet, meadow rue (*Thalictrum*), larkspur (*Delphinium*), monkshood (*Aconitum carmichaelii* and *A. fischeri* 'Wilsonii'), jewelweed or soldier's helmet (*Impatiens* spp.), and some delicately nodding columbine (*Aquilegia formosa*, *A. caerulea*, and *A. chrysantha*). Add lots of woodland ferns: evergreen wood fern (*Dryopteris*) and Christmas

fern (*Polystichum acrostichoides*), both stay green even in subzero temperatures; royal ferns (*Osmunda regalis*), interrupted ferns (*O. claytoniana*), oak ferns (*Gymnocarpium dryopteris*), maidenhair (*Adiantum* spp.), lady fern (*Athyrium filix-femina*), hay-scented ferns (*Dennstaedtia punctilobula*), golden-back fern (*Pityrogramma triangularis*), chain fern (*Woodwardia*), spleenwort (*Asplenium*), cliff brake (*Pellaea*), all look pretty. Because most of these shrubs and flowers bloom sequentially from early spring into fall, the garden always has something—and often several somethings—in bloom,

Lady fern (Athyrium filix-femina) *likes the rich, damp soil of a stream bank or a shady woods where it spreads rapidly, a delightful characteristic in an attractive plant.*

except in the dead of winter. Because many of the plants mentioned are native wildflowers, they will pretty well take care of themselves, self-sowing year after year. With daphne, daffodils, narcissus, violets, and lily-of-the-valley this garden could be famous for fragrance. It would be a daily pleasure to wend one's way along a stone path that wound its way through the woods to the front door.

So why does anyone plant a front lawn?

ON THE SUBJECT OF LAWNS

The front lawn is an American obsession. Billions of dollars are spent every year on seed and sod, sprinkler systems and aerators, lawn food and fertilizers, herbicides and pesticides, lawn mowers and dethatchers, edgers and leaf rakes, and heaven knows what else.

Some communities have ordinances specifying how high the grass may grow before the law steps in. What happens if, perish the thought, one travels, and the lawn grows too long? Is the returning traveler greeted at the curb by hundreds of incensed citizens fiercely wagging their fingers? Is one fined for every inch over the allowable limit? Is it permissible to trim one's lawn down barely below the level specified in an ordinance and still be within the law? Will the neighbors turn their backs on you at the block party? How did the lawn get this grip on the American consciousness?

The money spent annually on lawn care is nothing next to that spent trying to find grasses that will approximate AstroTurf® as closely as possible. The grass must be dense, it must take foot traffic, it must feel good underfoot, and above all, it must be green year-round. This is a major

Lawns are the most common landscape feature in American residential landscaping, in spite of the fact that it is nearly impossible to grow a lawn that is green year-round in most parts of the United States.

challenge in most of the United States. In fact, Washington and Oregon are the only two states that can reliably produce good lawns year-round, and two states out of fifty is a pretty poor percentage. (In California, where one's tan determines to a large extent one's social *cachet*, it is rumored that people in the Pacific Northwest don't tan, they rust, which will give you some idea of how much natural moisture is required to maintain a green lawn.) No grass I know of will survive freezing. Few will fail to turn brown in the arid and semiarid West and Southwest without the application of shameful amounts of water. *Sunset* magazine once ran an article on how Westerners might go about spray painting their lawn green to make it look

something other than dead in the summer. In a country where I have seen plastic flowers stuck in a border out of bloom, I suppose painting the lawn green falls within the law, but frankly, I'd hesitate to call it gardening.

Walter Doty, one of the most knowledgeable men ever to mess around in the morass of popular horticulture, loved lawns. He thought they were wonderful places for children to run through the sprinklers on a hot summer afternoon. He is also the man who transformed *Sunset* from a literary magazine that published the likes of Jack London and Bret Harte into one of the most influential house and garden magazines in the nation. When Walter reached his seventies, *Sunset* retired him. Walter didn't like that, so he promptly started writing and editing garden books for Ortho. I was lucky enough to work with him on some of those books. We argued a lot over whether the pleasures of lawns are worth the work. Walter thought they were; I had my doubts.

When Walter got his second pacemaker sometime in his eighties, Ortho forcibly retired him. Walter refused to take such nonsense lying down. Instead he founded Horticultural Publishing (HP Books), a series of excellent gardening books that competed very successfully with both Ortho and *Sunset*, right on through his third pacemaker and into his nineties. My ambition is to grow up to be just like Walter Doty. But I still think lawns are more work and more expense than they're worth, and dull as dust besides.

I wish Walter were still around. I'd like to hear what he thinks of some of my alternatives, even though he'd probably snort.

The tradition of immaculate lawns came to America from dear, damp England where it rains or is cloudy every month of the year—conditions that are hard to duplicate in America.

© Michael Landis

WHAT TO DO WITH WHAT YOU'VE GOT

I T IS DIFFICULT TO SAY WHICH CHILDHOOD influences have directed the turnings of one's life, what casual remark may lead to a lifetime fascination. Still, if one's ideas, beliefs, quirks, and absorbing passions must be attributed to a specific source, I would say that many of mine came from reading books written for children several generations before me. While others of my age were reading Carolyn Keene (Nancy Drew mysteries) and Walter Farley (*The Black Stallion*), I was reading Frances Hodgson Burnett, author of *The Secret Garden*. Through her two characters, Mary and Colin, I learned about the healing power of gardens.

The Secret Garden is the story of three children who find a walled garden so long locked and abandoned that it is difficult to imagine except in its over-

© Michael Landis

Ivy spills over the back of one of the little flagstone benches built into the terraces in the lower garden at Hillside House (seen in the previous photograph). It is an excellent place to sip a cup of tea and peruse leather-bound copies of Shirley Hibbard's Victorian magazine, **Floral World.**

grown state. In the process of restoring the garden the children, too, grow and blossom. I loved that story and I loved the idea of restoring to beauty and usefulness a long-neglected garden. But before I could find the garden of refuge I daydreamed about, many things intervened—marriage, children, college, graduate school, divorce, and writing. As my children learned to read, I gave each *The Secret Garden*, and delighted in their pleasure. And then, ten years ago, I found my own secret garden.

It is in California, in what the *Sunset New Western Garden Book* calls "one of the finest horticultural climates in Northern California." It

might as well have said, "one of the finest horticultural climates in the world," for that is what it is. The house itself is pretty and pleasant, a two-story brown shingle summer cottage built at the turn of the century. In the early years of its life, it helped house survivors of the great San Francisco earthquake of 1906. They came by ferry and train and carriage, fleeing the earthquake and fire that left San Francisco a city of rubble and ashes.

But it was not the house and its history that drew me to the place; it was the stone terraces and graciously curving flagstone walks that wind their way down the hill. It was the huge native oaks that created a canopy of filtered shade; it was the little stone benches built into the terraces of the lower garden. It was the thirty years of neglect that turned what had once been a showplace—the first owners used to bring hundreds of flats of summer annuals over on the ferry from San Francisco for the Chinese houseboy to plant —into a jungle of blackberry (*Rubus*) bramble, Scotch broom (*Cytisus scoparius*), and poison oak (*Rhus diversiloba*). I loved it from the first moment I saw it.

It was a daunting prospect. Even the cultivated plants had run wild. Periwinkle (*Vinca major*) and ivy (*Hedera canariensis*) had joined forces with the weeds to the point that the paths were so completely overgrown that I found one set of flagstone steps by simply falling down them: The mass of vegetation and oak leaf duff was so thick I hadn't even known the steps were there. It occurred to me, as I ruefully rubbed my knee, that flagstone is not a native stone, certainly not in the form of neat steps, and further investigation established that a flagged walk descended the hill all the way to a gate that was once the main entrance to the house.

The first chore was to plunge into a frenzy of cutting and clearing in order to determine at least the

English ivy, Algerian ivy, periwinkle, and white-flowered Allium triquetum *tumble over the stone terraces, forming a ground cover around the rhododendrons, hawthorn, and cotoneaster.*

© Michael Landis

basic outline and dimensions of the old garden. An ancient boxwood hedge stood nearly ten feet high and appeared to be mostly dead. The ivy had headed up the trunks of the venerable oaks in search of new territory. A little white flowered allium (*Allium triquetrum*) the children call "onion flower" declared itself queen of the garden, carpeting the ground and growing in the stone walls, between the flags of the paths, even popping up out of the leaf duff that covered the old stone barbecue. Pulling it made the air sting of raw onion until our eyes watered.

My original ambition was to clear enough of the mess to see where the stone terraces began and ended, and to clear one terrace down to the soil in order to put in bare-root roses. I anticipated spending one day at it. The garden had other plans. I had failed to give proper consideration to the fact that the periwinkle, blackberry, and ivy were inextricably tangled together, and that they had long since overrun the bounds of the terraces where they had originally taken root. A branch of ivy that began on one terrace might end forty feet away, having covered most of two other terraces and climbed halfway up a tree *en route*. In other words, it was not a one-day project, and I did not clear just one terrace. With the help of an inexplicably loyal and hardworking friend, the man

The flagstone steps from the patio to the lower garden are bordered by yellow archangel on one side and a low boxwood hedge on the other. The little white snowdrop-shaped **Allium** *pops up everywhere in the spring.*

© Michael Landis

who is now my husband, we ended up clearing the entire backyard.

At the time, we made a decision that appeared to reek of thoughtfulness and good sense. Something had to be done with the detritus of our efforts. The choices were to either stuff it in approximately a million leaf bags and trot it up sixty steps, whence it might be hauled off to the dump, or to consider the law of gravity (down is almost always faster and easier than up) and declare the bottommost terrace the town's biggest compost heap. A farsighted vision of utter exhaustion prevailed and we opted for the compost heap. Thirty years of periwinkle, ivy, blackberry canes as thick as my wrist, and oak leaf duff were dropped into that twelve-foot-by-thirty-foot terrace, and I have had cause to regret it ever since. Every blessed scrap happily took root in the rich, black duff, and I've been trying to clear the accursed stuff out of that terrace for ten years now.

A 'Hachiya' persimmon tree in the lower garden has soft, pale green leaves in spring, yellow and orange leaves in the fall, and golden fruit in winter. It was nearly eaten alive by the English ivy at its base, but cutting the ivy down allowed both to live in peaceful coexistence.

OF THE ROSE AND THE STAG

It is hard for me now to realize the innocence with which I undertook the restoration of a seventy-five-year-old garden. Perhaps it is better that I had then no clue as to the nature and dimensions of the task. I recently ran across the list of the first roses I put in. I chose the best All-American Rose Selections (AARS), and what high hopes I had for them! 'Honor', 'Pascali', and 'White Masterpiece' for whites; 'Peace', 'Oregold', and 'Sutter's Gold' for yellows; 'Mister Lincoln', 'Proud Land', 'Red Masterpiece', 'Snowfire' (a bicolor that is white on the outside, red on the inside), and 'Double Delight' (which is the reverse bicolor, red on the outside, white on the inside) for reds; and a passel of the prettiest pinks: 'Queen Elizabeth' (which is

far and away my favorite rose), 'Tiffany' for fragrance, 'Pristine', and 'First Prize'. All rated highly on color, form, growth habit, and disease- and pest-resistance. But the roses had no resistance to the pest I had the most of, and for years the deer browsed those roses to pitiful stubs. In six years I don't think I had more than one rose a year that escaped the deer.

I sprayed with deer repellant, which worked until the rain washed it off. I bought lion dung from the zoo and festooned the roses like thorny little Christmas trees with white cheesecloth bags. I surrounded each rose with a chicken wire cage. I let a large dog run loose in the yard. I fenced, and grew ivy on the fence to make it appear even higher and more impenetrable. The deer ate the ivy, too. I shouted at the deer from the sun-room windows; the deer merely looked at me as though I were lamentably ill-bred. Here is what I learned about controlling deer damage: Everything works for a little while, and nothing works for long.

Eventually I accepted reality, and ripped out six dozen roses. I planted rhododendrons and azaleas instead. The deer don't seem to like rhododendrons, which has a lot to do with why I do. A magnificent six-point buck has been strolling the grounds lately, but so far he hasn't touched the rhododendrons.

WATER, WATER, EVERYWHERE

In the process of clearing we stumbled across a brass sprinkler head that led us to the discovery of an elaborate sprinkler system. As we pulled and pruned and trimmed and raked we wondered whether it worked or could be made to work again. While I planted roses, my friend traced the pipes (by tearing up some of the flagstone) to a complicated five-valve control buried under three feet of mud. It took two more days before it was all working, but since then one or any combination of terraces or the whole garden may be watered with a twist of the wrist.

WAIT A YEAR TO SEE WHAT'S THERE

Looking at the list of things I put in at the beginning, I see that the choices were good. I planted roses and bulbs, always the sturdiest of troopers. Wherever there has been an old garden, these are

© Michael Landis

'Loder's White' rhododendrons bloom spectacularly in the filtered light under the Coast live oaks in the upper garden.

the ones that survive to tell the tale, along with lilacs (*Syringa*) and bearded iris (*Iris* x *germanica*). I put in 150 daffodils, mostly the classic yellow 'King Alfred', and the white 'Mount Hood' and 'Thalia', plus some miniatures; 150 Dutch iris (*Iris xiphium*), fifty crocus tucked in stone walls and under oaks, and species tulips (*Tulipa* spp.) along the paths. Still, I know now that the trees needed to be trimmed to let in more light. After the first year's show, the bulbs came up blind until the trees were opened up. The ground covers were too aggressive for tiny bulbs like crocus, miniature daffodils and species tulips; the larger bulbs were able to rise above them. Now I know.

If I were a good and patient gardener, I would have waited a year before planting anything, both to discover what was already there and to get a better idea of climate and soil conditions in order to more accurately predict what would do well. But patience is a quality of those more saint-like than I.

That first spring was a delight to behold. The oaks leafed out in bright pink before shading into green. The plum (*Prunus*) thicket looked like a sea of white froth. The hawthorns and cherries and plums were masses of white blossoms. An immense sweet mock orange (*Philadelphus coronarius*) scented the whole front garden. The tall, silver-leafed cotoneaster brought a graceful fountain of tiny white flowers to the celebration of spring. The little allium carpeted the ground with nodding, white, bell-shaped flowers. The whole garden looked like a wedding cake. Sixty years before Vita Sackville-West wrote in her *Garden Book* (1968) of the white garden she created at Sissinghurst, someone had planted a white garden at Hillside.

THE GROUND COVER QUEEN

Over the years, more daffodils have been tucked under the periwinkle and wandering Jew (*Trades-*

The nodding, white, bell-like flowers of the **Allium triquetum** *are the first sign that winter has ended at Hillside House. It has naturalized, and thousands bloom to welcome spring each year.*

© Michael Landis

© Michael Landis

Kenilworth ivy makes a delicate tracery against the stone walls of the terraces.

cantia albiflora). A pretty little white wood sorrel (*Oxalis purpurea* [*O. variabilis*]) appeared along the paths and Kenilworth ivy (*Cymbalaria muralis*) volunteered to clamber up the stone walls. A slope of hopeless clay and rubble on which a dozen different species had died a dreadful death finally disappeared under silver-and-green-leaved yellow archangel *Lamiastrum galeobdolon* (often sold as *Lamium* in nurseries). The trimmings of ground covers from one place were carefully rooted in another until the bare places began to vanish.

There is a widely held belief among my family and friends that I am mortally offended by bare dirt. This is reflected in the fact that my son has on occasion introduced me as the "ground cover queen of California," and certainly it is undeniable that I like the look of green and lots of it. *Sunset* once came out to look at my garden as a possible story on restoring an old garden; the associate garden editor murmured that perhaps a story on ground covers might be more appropriate.

Practically everything grows through something else. Calla lilies emerge, tall and regal, through wandering Jew. Both white and blue lily-of-the-Nile (*Agapanthus orientalis*) rise up out of the yellow archangel. Summer lilies and asparagus (*Asparagus*) poke up past the strawberries (*Fragaria*). The periwinkle must be brushed out of the Japanese maples and azaleas every now and again. The persimmon tree (*Diospyros kaki* 'Hachiya') had to be rescued from the English ivy (*Hedera helix*) that nearly smothered it, the fact that the persimmon stood some fifteen feet tall notwithstanding. The Hall's Japanese honeysuckle (*Lonicera japonica* 'Halliana') must be constantly persuaded to climb the fence and not root itself promiscuously wherever it touches the earth in the back garden, and the star jasmine (*Trachelospermum jasminoides*) is subject to the same persistent persuasion in the front. This is not a garden for the terminally tidy.

© Michael Landis

A calla lily blooms against a background of white Oxalis.

© Michael Landis

This pretty little Oxalis *grows well in niches between the rocks of the stone terraces. This much vilified family has suffered in reputation from the aggressive manner of its one weed, the red* O. corniculata, *but the others are quite charming and easy to grow.*

Despite their wandering ways, ground covers actually help keep the garden looking orderly. The backyard has three immense deciduous oaks (*Quercus kelloggii*, *Q. lobata*), and the front yard has two evergreen California live oaks (*Q. agrifolia*). "Evergreen" here means they shed leaves all year, especially in the spring instead of only in the fall. The ground covers absorb their leaves silently and efficiently. The daffodils are set off attractively by the dark green ivy, and when they reach that embarrassing phase where they are past bloom but the leaves must be left to set next year's bud, the ivy discreetly covers it up. The Kenilworth ivy joined forces with the wandering Jew and silver-leaved yellow archangel to turn an ugly rubble wall into a delicate tapestry of pretty leaves and tiny flowers, entirely masking the ugly chunks of concrete and broken brick. Best of all, I can have lots of trees, and rarely have to rake.

Most books declare that ground covers compete with other garden plants for water and growing space, but that has not been my experience at all. Rather, they give the rhododendrons, azaleas, camellias, and Japanese maples the cool root run they need to thrive. Thick ground covers keep the soil shaded and moist. I'm convinced that it requires less water to maintain shrubs in ground cover than in either lawns or bare soil, simply because so much less is lost to evaporation and runoff. Just think of ground covers as living mulch.

Because conserving water is essential in California—no, in the twentieth century—watering is done in the evening or on cloudy days when

'Loder's White' rhododendrons combine well with pink and white variegated azaleas 'California Sunset' and 'Gloria' in the upper terraces. The ground covers spilling over the walls include periwinkle, ivy, yellow archangel, and wandering Jew. They help keep the soil cool and moist.

© Michael Landis

cooler temperatures let the plants make the best use of water, and the soil is not baked hard so that it doesn't absorb anything. Because the soil is always cool and shaded, the garden never needs the deep soaking that lawns require, that excess of water that so often kills native oaks adapted to going nine months of the year without rain.

OF SUN AND SHADE

When I first began working on the garden I was bursting with plans for all the things I'd grow: peonies (*Paeonia* spp.), masses of them; tomatoes (*Lycopersicon* spp.) by the bushel; herbs enough to use, dry, and make wreaths of; roses by the terraceful. The fact is that with trees comes shade. Peonies, tomatoes, and herbs need sun. With deer there can be no roses. That is what is meant by working with what you've got.

If you plant tomatoes in the shade, you'll get stringy vines and no tomatoes. Plant potatoes (*Solanom tuberosom*) instead. Or peas (*Pisum*), lettuces (*Lactuca*), broccoli (*Brassica oleracea*), or chard. If, on the other hand, you have blazing sun at midday, don't plant impatiens or cyclamen. They'll fry. One of the best pieces of horticultural advice ever given was the gift of Thalassa Crusoe in *Making Things Grow*: Find out what you can grow well and grow lots of it. That's why I grow rhododendrons, azaleas, camellias, Japanese maples, heavenly bamboo (*Nandina domestica*), thousands of bulbs, and a gang of ground covers: they all do well in filtered shade.

In the one place where there is plenty of sun, on the patio, there are oranges, lemons, limes, and tangerines in big terra-cotta pots. A small collection of herbs in a strawberry pot provides all the fresh oregano (*Origanum vulgare*), sweet marjoram (*O. majorana*), thyme (*Thymus vulgaris*), chives (*Allium schoenoprasum*), sage (*Salvia officinalis*), tarragon (*Artemisia dracunculus*), parsley, basil (*Ocimum basilicum*), and winter savory (*Satureja montana*) required for cooking. Another terra-cotta pot holds a twenty-year-old bush of rosemary to complete the culinary collection. I can pretty much grow what I want to, but on a smaller scale.

Oaks, maples, cherries, plums, apples, and hawthorns grow well in my garden, so I grow lots of them: three kinds of oaks, three kinds of maples, three kinds of cherries, four kinds of plums, two kinds of apples, and two large hawthorns. Healthy plants require a minimum of attention; one can devote one's time to enjoying them instead.

MEET CÉCILE BRUNNER

In my absolute determination to have roses, I planted climbing 'Cécile Brunner' (1881), a pale pink polyantha that was one of the first hybrid roses ever introduced. Climbing roses like having their feet in the shade and their heads in the sun. I guess I didn't really expect it to do well, because I plunked it in a big plastic bucket over soil best described as thoroughly sodden: A small spring runs underground there. I meant to build a proper planter for Cécile, but I didn't get around to it. I meant to buy a proper arch for her, too, but the only one available at the nursery that day was an inexpensive redwood arch, scarcely as sturdy as lath. But it gave the effect I wanted, so in it went.

Anyone who knows roses will tell you that you can't give a rose too much water. They will also tell you that a rose won't stand for wet feet, one of those deliciously descriptive anthropomorphic phrases that so accurately reflect plant behavior.

This is the view that greets anyone walking out the front door in early spring at Hillside House (above). Azaleas and rhododendrons provide a splash of pink and white against the green of the ground covers and the oak ferns that grow between the stones of the terraces. Overhead tower the Coast live oaks.

Japanese maples (left) have graceful, delicate foliage and they make a superb understory in a woodland garden, particularly under ancient oaks.

The sweetheart rose or baby rose is properly named 'Cécile Brunner', and it was one of the first hybrid roses, introduced in 1881.

In fact, the correct term for a rose that won't grow because it has wet feet is *sulking*. What this means in plain English is that you can pour all the water you want on a rose so long as it drains away immediately, leaving the soil with plenty of moisture and plenty of oxygen.

Time passed and the wandering Jew covered up the plastic bucket until it was invisible. The arch wasn't exactly solid, but it wasn't exactly collapsing, either. The rose grew nicely the first year. And then it went crazy. Suddenly the canes were two inches around. Suddenly new canes seemed to spring up once a week. Suddenly the canes grew ten, twenty, thirty feet long. And every inch was covered with tiny, exquisitely shaped pink rosebuds. Sprays of roses flung themselves over the oleander into the birch on one side, and onto the roof on the other. The house took on the appearance of a Nantucket 'Sconset cottage without the wall and roof trellises. Having never intended such a thing, I was unexpectedly made the delighted owner of a rose-covered cottage.

As it had never been fed or fertilized, this wild growth left me somewhat taken aback. The mystery was finally pieced together when I remembered the invisible plastic bucket. The rose had grown through the bottom, giving it access to all the water and nutrients it had ever hoped or dreamed of while the roots still in the pot had all the necessary oxygen. My laziness resulted in a paradise for roses, a paradise of roses.

Now, of course, Cécile is far too massive for the rickety redwood arch. It will have to be replaced with a sturdy metal arch like the ones at Wisley, the Royal Horticultural Society's garden outside London. The redwood one will have to be sawed apart and dismantled piece by piece. Somehow the huge rose canes must be supported in the process. It is a ghastly prospect. Perhaps I'll do it another day.

© Michael Landis

The pretty, wanton 'Cécile Brunner' busily turning a California shingle-style summer house into a rose-covered cottage, with long sprays flung onto the roof and others framing the French doors.

CHAPTER FOUR

THE URBANE URBAN VINE

F OR SOME REASON WE ASSOCIATE VINES with the country, as though they would not grow in cities. This is madness, of course. Vines grow perfectly well in cities, but the vine-covered cottage is a cliché of language and landscaping, with all that implies of the rural countryside. It is no less a cliché to perceive city gardening as confined to window boxes, though there is not the slightest horticultural imperative for doing so. Farms have fields, suburbs have lawns and trees, cities have traffic, noise, flashing neon lights, dirty air, sidewalks, a few hostage houseplants, and a dusty window box or two. What arrant nonsense.

There is not a city in the world that would not be vastly improved by planting trees along most of its major streets and all of the residential ones. Oh, but

Vines grow splendidly in cities, some reaching over porches like the climbing hydrangea on the previous page, some softening the urban skyline in a rooftop garden.

trees would interfere with power lines or truck traffic at the top and buckle sidewalks at the bottom, the city managers protest. Then put utility lines underground where they belong; they're a form of visual pollution anyway. Widen streets to accommodate the trees or reroute trucks onto freeways. Think of solutions, don't whine about the problems. Give beauty the same priority as function, and cool the earth and clean up the air at the same time, since that's what trees and other green things do for a living.

The purpose here is to shatter the clichés, to take a fresh look at what can grow where. Just as the suburban lawn may function more effectively as a small woods or a flowering meadow, there is no reason that the paved expanse of the city cannot blossom with trees and vines and shrubs. What if, for example, gentrification implied planting green vines to set off the brass carriage lamp on the front of a brownstone as certainly as it assumes refinishing the floors or stripping paint off the original moldings? What if, along with running water and functioning sewers, the city supplied every building with a tree to plant before the door? What if every dry cleaner, shoe repair shop, and supermarket had planters full of flowers out front? What if baskets of flowers hung from every lamppost in spring and summer as they do in Victoria, British Columbia? What if pots of bright flowers were displayed on the fronts of houses as they are in Spain? What if every neighborhood and township and borough had a Green Czar whose job it was to make every vacant lot a vest-pocket park, a garden refuge? What if every corner had one sidewalk paver removed so a single well-shaped evergreen arborvitae (*Thuja*) might grow?

Walter Doty once told me a story about Palo Alto, a suburb of San Francisco, close to where he lived. Many years ago the city council voted to plant trees along all the streets, both commercial and residential, and proceeded to do so. The trees

flourished, the people looking after them as though they were their own. When a tree was broken or died the people replaced it with another, and Palo Alto is today a community of lovely tree-lined streets.

East Palo Alto was planted at the same time, but the trees were not cared for. Most of the people there had little money, and what little they had went to feed their children, not replace city trees. Trees that were broken stayed broken; trees that died were eventually removed. Today the dividing line between Palo Alto and East Palo Alto is as clear as if there were a barbed wire fence between them. Palo Alto has trees and a sense of graciousness; East Palo Alto looks like a moonscape by comparison. The climate is the same; the soil is the same; the sun shines equally on both. But Palo Alto has beautiful old trees, and that makes all the difference.

THE URBANE VINE

Urban gardens differ from their suburban and rural counterparts in nearly every particular. Sometimes the only available space to garden is a rooftop or a balcony or a cramped space between tall buildings. Half the solution is to plant in containers: window boxes, planters, and pots. The other half of the solution is to think vertically. Vines, do, after all, both grow up and drape down.

If you have no place to garden but the bottom of an air shaft, think of it as a walled garden. Vines soften the look of walls. Boston ivy (*Parthenocissus tricuspidata*) and Virginia creeper (*P. quinquefolia*) make a lovely green tracery across a wall, and both turn a splendid scarlet in the fall. Climbing hydrangea (*Hydrangea anomala* subsp. *petiolaris*) is hardy, grows fast, and has white lace-cap flowers too; all it asks is plenty of water and something to

© Charles Mann

Boston ivy is a classic urban vine, the famous ivy of the Ivy League. The men in my family habitually attend Yale, and when my grandmother escorted the first of her grandsons to college, she remarked that the ivy appeared to be the only thing holding the buildings up.

hold onto. Common trumpet creeper (*Campsis radicans*) is native to the eastern United States. If it gets frozen to the ground, it comes back from the roots. A rambunctious dark green vine that grows enthusiastically to forty feet with loose clusters of large orange and red flowers, trumpet creeper looks positively tropical. English ivy grows more slowly, but it stays green all year. In places where it's warm enough, plant Algerian ivy (*Hedera canariensis*) or creeping fig (*Ficus pumila*.) All of these vines cling to walls by themselves.

The idea is to conceive of skyscrapers entirely differently—think of it as Trump's Trellis instead of Trump Tower, and you'll have the concept. Tall buildings are not merely walls to live within, but structures to plant on. The goal is to achieve cities of living walls, rich with green leaves and bright with flowers, to give the phrase "the greening of America" a whole new meaning.

Walls are warmer than the air because of heat lost from the interior of the building, because they absorb heat from the sun, and because they give protection from bitter winds. In medieval times fruits like apricots (*Prunus armeniala*), peaches (*P. persica*), and pears (*Pyrus communis*) were espaliered against the walls of the cloister so the warmth of the wall would ripen the fruit. Vines that won't thrive out in the open may do well against a wall. If there is no soil in which to plant them, put them in large containers the size of half-barrels. Be forewarned that clinging vines, while a joy and a delight because they needn't be wired to the wall tendril by tendril, can be a headache of migraine proportions if they must be taken down.

The effect of vines on the appearance of high-rise buildings can be quite startling. It is my observation that much of American residential architecture of the last fifty years is, to put the point gently, undistinguished. That's why there is such a desperate nationwide desire for old houses with generous rooms, fireplaces, wood floors, wainscoting, attics, basements, and dormered roofs. In the fifties, housing tracts were flung up as fast as the developer could frame, building block after block of identical houses. In the pricier developments, there was a choice of five different façades and floor plans to choose from, the five repeated endlessly. Multistory apartment buildings were no more than rectangles with windows.

Today, several widely read national magazines exist for the sole purpose of showing people how modern bungalows can be furnished to look like an eighteenth-century colonial cottage or a nineteenth-century Southern mansion or almost anything except a twentieth-century bungalow. I submit that it is easier to make a tract house appear to have old-fashioned charm with trees and vines and shrubs and flowers than with an authentic Appalachian rocker artfully draped with an Amish quilt in front of sliding glass doors.

A case in point: Not long ago I went to Los Angeles to spend some time in Westwood, near the University of California, Los Angeles, and stayed at a hotel that described itself as charmingly European. So indeed it was, with trees and flowers all around and covered with creeping fig. It took me several moments to recognize the old International Student House that had been home to many of my friends when I was a graduate student at the university. I was not especially sur-

Creeping fig is an extremely dense self-clinging vine that does a superb job of blotting out dull architecture.

Trumpet creeper is a fast-growing, summer-blooming vine that clings to brick, wood, or stucco with aerial rootlets. It's native to the northeastern United States.

prised to see that the old Rec Room, in which many a hotly contested, hard-fought international Ping-Pong game was played, had become a handsome conference room, but I was frankly astonished by how appealingly the trees and vines had softened and transformed the appearance of an architecturally uninspired student dormitory into an elegant hotel.

Surely the same thing could be done with similarly undistinguished apartment buildings in other cities. Surely many of the identical tract homes that march rank and file across the American landscape could cover themselves with glory by masking their painfully ordinary lines with some well-kept vines. The term for doing so in horticultural circles is *planting out*, which means nothing more than making things you don't want to look at disappear behind the foliage. John McLaren, the crusty Scotsman responsible for turning windswept sand dunes into the urban jewel that is today Golden Gate Park in San Francisco, was a master of the technique. He also loathed commemorative statuary. Every time the city council insisted on putting another bronze horseman in the park, he planted shrubs and trees around it until it was virtually invisible. In perfect honesty, it must be admitted that in the end the city council took its revenge: When McLaren died, they erected a statue of him in Golden Gate Park.

In All Their Glory

Vines can contribute more than mere foliage to the project of improving a four-way view of walls in a small urban garden. Lots of vines flower splendidly. It is old-fashioned and often not available unless you take cuttings yourself, but there are few happier horticultural effects than morning-glory spilling over a wall, tumbling over a garden gate, or cascading across a front porch. Use the peren-

nial morning-glory blue dawn flower (*Ipomoea acuminata* [*I. leari*]), that opens bright blue and fades to pink by evening. Most nurseries don't sell it because it's rampant; I think that's one of its greatest charms.

The annual morning-glories found in seed packets have bigger flowers in more colors, but they're a one-shot deal, lasting only a single summer. It would be fun to combine the annual and perennial morning-glories along a rambling fence, the white moonflower (*I. alba*) with the rare large-flowered Imperial Japanese morning-glories (*I. nil* and *I. tricolor*), which may be funnel-shaped or bell-like, single or double, bicolored, solid, or striped. However, annual morning-glory seeds have to be abraded with a file, nicked with a knife, or soaked in warm water for two days, or the silly things refuse to sprout.

Vines cover a multitude of sins so effectively that I have occasionally entertained the thought of simply planting some at my feet and standing still. Ugly stumps, sagging barns, ratty fences, junked cars, and run-down buildings all disappear, lost in a mass of flowers when vines are planted over them. Flowering vines may be the most effective and attractive approach to urban renewal currently available. Just think how the inner cities might be improved in only a year or two if every tenement were covered over with ivy or concealed from view by a cascade of flowers. And if the views are ugly, as they often are in slums, why, grow the vines right over the windows to give even the most dismal cold-water walk-up the feeling of a bower.

The Accomplice Vine

There was an Agatha Christie mystery in which silver lace vine (*Polygonum aubertii*) figured prominently as the key to solving the murder. Also known as mile-a-minute vine, it had been planted

Silver lace vine (right) *is the ultimate fast fix, horticulturally speaking. It can cover one hundred square feet in a single season, is covered with frothy white blooms from summer to fall, and ordinances should be drafted requiring that it be planted on all unattractive buildings within city limits.*

This annual morning-glory (Ipomoea tricolor) (below) *blooms all summer in splendid profusion. Its perennial cousin, blue dawn flower* (I. acuminata), *does the same, but comes back year after year.*

over the victim's grave and looked so established that who would have suspected that it had been put in but a few months before? But Miss Marple knew silver lace vine can cover one hundred square feet in a single season, and the jig was up in no time. It did seem rather a shame to tear out a thriving vine to retrieve the corpse, though.

Given warm enough weather, silver lace vine is evergreen; otherwise, it's deciduous. It can be pruned to the ground without harm every year, but then it won't bloom again until August. Better to live with the mass of thatch through the winter (the snow will cover it anyway) and have its frothy, creamy bloom from May to October.

CLASSIC ELEGANCE

Wisteria (*Wisteria*) is one of the classic vines, and one of the most beautiful. It lives longer than most people, and gets huge, so give it solid support from the beginning. In urban gardens, build a sturdy arbor between the walls to sit under so you can look up and see the flowers. Wisteria will shade, scent, and delight the soul all summer, color clear yellow in the fall, and let in light in winter, too. The silvery gray twisted trunk is as beautiful as the flowers—it has the same sense of character and strength as century-old olive trees.

Chinese wisteria (*Wisteria sinensis*) blooms in pale blue or white, and hangs in spectacular, lightly fragrant clusters. Japanese wisteria (*W. floribunda*) has a broader range of colors—white, pink, and several shades of blue, lavender, and purple marked with yellow and white. It also stays in bloom longer because the cluster doesn't flower all at once. Most wisteria clusters are eighteen inches long, but Japanese wisteria 'Longissima' has violet clusters three feet long; 'Longissima Alba', has white flowers two feet long. Japanese wisteria does best in full sun, while Chinese wisteria blooms in

Purple wisteria has spectacular flowers in spring, clear yellow color in autumn, and a sense of tremendous strength and character to the silvery-gray twisted trunk and branches in winter.

considerable shade. Silky wisteria (*W. venusta*) has pale, silky hairs on its leaves, and very large white or purple-blue flowers hanging in short, chubby clusters. Plant it in full sun and it will flower in mad profusion just as the leaves begin to open in early spring.

Young wisteria needs plenty of food and water, but established plants look better with less. They bloom more profusely grown hard—that is, the more difficult the conditions the more they thrive.

SUMMER SHOW

If you're landscaping a fancywork wrought iron balcony in the French Quarter of New Orleans, get three big pots and plant evergreen clematis (*Clematis armandii*) in one, *C. lanuginosa* 'Candida'

White wisteria is striking grown over a veranda or along the eaves. A vine this magnificent sets off a handsome house beautifully, and renders unremarkable architecture virtually invisible.

Clematis like this one are a true joy: plant them once and they bloom every year in fine profusion. They come in a range of colors from white to blue to purple to red to yellow. This one is C. lawsoniana *'Henryi'.*

and *C.l.* 'Duchess of Edinburgh' in another, and *C. Lawsoniana* 'Henryi' and *C.l.* 'Prince Philip' in the third. All of these bloom white, except 'Prince Philip', which has immense, royal purple flowers ten inches across. They will flower successively: *C. armandii* and 'Candida' in March and April, 'Duchess of Edinburgh' in May and June, 'Prince Philip', June through August, and 'Henryi', June through September. 'Candida' blooms again in

July, and 'Duchess of Edinburgh' blooms a second time in September.

Just these five plants give bloom from March to September, with a spectacular show in mid-summer when 'Candida', 'Duchess of Edinburgh', 'Prince Philip', and 'Henryi' all bloom simultaneously. 'Candida' has eight-inch blooms, 'Duchess of Edinburgh' has six-inch double flowers, 'Henryi' has eight-inch flowers, and 'Prince Philip', breathtaking ten-inch blooms. The thick, dark green leaves of the evergreen clematis hide the thin, wiry stems of the others after their leaves drop, so the balcony looks pretty all year, even when nothing's in bloom.

If you don't have a filigreed wrought-iron balcony, or don't live in New Orleans, plant clematis anyway, on the fire escape, if that's all the space there is. It's too good a show to miss. Burn the cut stems of the flowers to make them last longer, and float them in a crystal bowl with pink rose petals. The pale, fluffy seed clusters are intriguing in flower arrangements.

THE DIVINE, ENTWINING EDIBLE VINE

For those who desire sustenance for the body as well as the soul from their gardens, there are two varieties of passionflower that not only have strange and striking flowers, but produce delectable fruit as well. Purple granadilla (*Passiflora edulis*) has two-inch purple-and-white flowers followed by three-inch dark purple or yellow fruits in the spring and fall. *P.* 'Incense' is even nicer because it smells like sweet peas, has five-inch violet flowers, and is evergreen. The yellow-green fruit is also richly fragrant.

The name, passionflower was bestowed on the plant by the Spanish missionaries who brought it

Strangely beautiful, passionflowers are always fascinating to look at, often fragrant, and some produce edible fruit as well.

out of South America. They used it to explain the Catholic mysteries to the native Indians they sought to convert, explaining that it symbolized Christ's passion on the cross. The fringe in the center of the flower represents the crown of thorns; the five stamens, the five wounds; and the petals, the Apostles who remained steadfast to the end.

If you live somewhere that gets good summer rain or can supply copious amounts of water, grow hops (*Humulus lupulus*). Just give them something to climb on and they'll try to take over the world between spring and summer. The hops themselves, flaky little conelike bracts, smell like fresh pine, and are used to flavor beer.

Hops grow up the veranda of an 1880 Queen Anne Victorian my husband's family has in Redstone, Colorado. The year we had a family reunion there, the hops grew faster than I could

twine them along the posts and rails of the porch that curved around the house. Grown over an arbor, hops create a place of cool, pine-sweet, pale green shade all summer. It sprouts in May and by midsummer is fifteen to twenty-five feet long. The new sprouts can be eaten as a vegetable, but if you do, you'll have eaten your summer shade.

Another delicious edible vine is the scarlet runner bean (*Phaseolus coccineus*). Like hops, it needs something to grow on—green string or wire will do. Put strings over a window and plant the beans at the bottom of the strings. You'll screen out the view, have bright red flowers to look at, and be able to pick beans for dinner without leaving the house. They're good harvested young like snap beans or picked when the pods are dry and eaten like green lima beans. The beans are wondrous, all splotched bright purple and cream.

Hops vines grow fast, the flowers smell like pine, and the Latin name is a tongue twister—Humulus lupulus.

The ultimate edible vine, *The Vine*, as it were, is the grape (*Vitis* spp.). It has beautiful leaves that make beautiful *dolmas* (stuffed grape leaves), it produces grapes for the table or for wine, it colors vibrantly in the fall, and it lives approximately forever. A single vine can produce enough new growth each year to form a leafy wall, arch a walk, or shade a terrace. Some years ago I lived briefly in a house where a 'Perlette' grapevine had been trained along the eaves of the house. It had also been planted directly over an abandoned septic tank, where it thrived. That summer it produced so many bunches that we gave grapes away in grocery bags to anyone who would take them.

THE FRAGRANT BOWER

Beyond foliage, beyond flowers, lies fragrance. Certainly the plant that first comes to mind when one thinks of fragrance is jasmine (*Jasminum* spp.), yet not all jasmines are fragrant, and one of the sweetest-smelling plants commonly called jasmine isn't really a jasmine at all: star jasmine (also known as Confederate jasmine) is a *Trachelospermum* (*Trachelospermum jasminoides* to be exact). Like evergreen clematis, star jasmine is slow getting started, then takes off in a rush with long shoots twining in every direction, eventually grow-

There is no other image that so perfectly bespeaks the richness and abundance of summer than ripe grapes on the vine.

Angel-wing jasmine is deliciously fragrant. It blooms best in hot climates.

olens]) is a deciduous vine with summer flowers that smell like gardenia. So why didn't they call it Chilean gardenia? Because gardenia is a shrub, and most jasmines are vines, except the one that's used to make all the fragrant jasmine-scented things most people are familiar with, which is a shrub, but they obviously intended to describe the plant's growth accurately, rather than its scent, which, as stated before, is like a gardenia. There. Is that clear? I'm twining both star jasmine and Chilean jasmine on the same deck railing in the hope that the star jasmine's evergreen leaves will cover up the bare stems of the Chilean jasmine in the winter. They are planted next to the front door, and if the scheme works, the fragrance greeting summer visitors at the door should be exquisite.

ing to twenty feet. The glossy, dark green leaves are pretty, the little clusters of white pinwheel-shaped flowers are attractive, but ultimately it is the fragrance that makes it worth growing. Let it twine itself up a porch, drape itself down a wall, or curl all over a trellis. Most important, plant it where you can enjoy its fragrance—beside a door, under a bedroom window, next to a much-used gate. This is *the* smell of warm summer nights.

The best jasmines for fragrance are poet's jasmine (*J. officinale*), angel-wing jasmine (*J. nitidum*), Spanish jasmine (*J. grandiflorum*), and *J. polyanthum*, which has flowers that are white on the inside and pink on the outside. The jasmine used in making teas, perfumes, and Hawaiian leis is pikake (*J. sambac*), which is not a vine, but a subtropical shrub. Just think how romantic a small courtyard would smell with two or three different jasmine in full bloom!

Chilean jasmine (*Mandevilla laxa* [*M. suave-*

Twined over a doorway or on a trellis near a window, star jasmine is the smell of warm summer evenings. It would be wonderfully romantic trellised up a courtyard wall.

Carolina Jessamine (or yellow jasmine) sounds like something Tom Robbins would name a Southern belle. It's pretty, it smells good, and all parts of it are poisonous.

Madagascar jasmine (*Stephanotis floribunda*) is an evergreen vine best known for its frequent appearance in bridal bouquets. If you lack the sub-tropical climate this needs to flourish, it will grow very happily as a houseplant in the winter; just put it outdoors when warm weather comes. Let it dry out before either taking it out or bringing it in. It blooms all summer grown outdoors; and again six weeks after being put outdoors from the house. The fragrance, as any bride can tell you, is purely lovely.

Carolina yellow jasmine (*Gelsemium semper-virens*) has masses of large, fragrant, yellow flowers that bloom in spring and again in the fall. It is evergreen with red stems and covers quickly.

No discussion of fragrance can leave out the honeysuckles (*Lonicera* spp.). Hall's honeysuckle perfumes the lower garden at my country house, though it must be frequently reminded that it is a climber, not a ground cover, as it is tucked back onto the fence. Hall's honeysuckle is the selfsame Japanese honeysuckle that is such a pest in the Northeastern United States, but the growing conditions are clearly less suitable in northern California. It is often recommended for tough situations such as steep, sunny slopes with poor soil. Planted on what was left after a major mud slide some years ago—subsoil on a forty-five degree angle with midday sun—it found the situation so difficult the poor plant reverted to juvenile leaves. A better choice for less moderate climates is everblooming honeysuckle (*Lonicera heckrottii*), which *The National Arborhetum Book of Outstanding Garden Plants* calls "the most beautiful of the climbing, twining types." The flowers open yellow, fade to pink, and attract ruby-throated hummingbirds all summer; the red berries attract songbirds in the fall. Woodbine (*L. periclymenum* 'Graham Thomas') grows to forty feet, has sweet-smelling yellow and white flowers that are fragrant until frost, and red fruits.

THE BIRDWATCHER'S CHOICE

My city friends often remark on all the birds at my house. They tell me there are no birds in the city except sparrows and pigeons. There are two reasons for that. The first is that there's not much for songbirds to eat in urban environments. The other is that most people don't recognize what they see. The first issue can be addressed by growing vines that flower (hummingbirds), fruit (songbirds), and provide places to perch and nest (all birds). The second issue is best addressed by a pair of binoculars and a good field guide such as Roger Tory Peterson's *Guide to the Birds* or The National Geographic Society's *Field Guide to the Birds of North America.*

Gold flame honeysuckle (Lonicera heckrottii) *grows vigorously and blooms freely from spring until frost.*

This is a hybrid between Chinese trumpet creeper (Campsis grandiflora) and common trumpet creeper (C. radicans) called C. x tagliabuana 'Mme. Galen.' It tolerates cold weather better than either of its parents.

There are nearly thirty species of sparrow found in North America, not counting the finches, longspurs, and buntings often mistaken for sparrows. It takes real skill and knowledge to identify the sparrows correctly, if you like challenges. There are more than a dozen species of pigeons—more properly called doves, including the city pigeon, which is a rock dove.

If you are lucky enough to live along a migratory route, there is the possibility of attracting a shifting kaleidescope of birds all year long. Vines that contribute to this effort by providing food and shelter are trumpet creeper (*Campsis grandiflora, C. radicans, C. x tagliabuana* 'Madame Galen'), bit-

tersweet (*Celastrus orbiculatus, C. scandens*), Carolina moonseed (*Cocculus carolinus*), scarlet kadsura (*Kadsura japonica*), coral greenbrier (*Smilax megalantha*), Small's brier (*S. lanceolata*), red-berried bamboo (*S. walteri*), porcelain ampelopsis (*Ampelopsis brevipedunculata*), wintercreeper (*Euonymus fortunei* 'Erecta'), woodbine (*Parthenocissus henryana, P. quinquefolia, P. tricuspidata*), honeysuckle (*Lonicera etrusca* 'Superba', *L. heckrottii, L. periclymenum* 'Graham Thomas', *L. sempervirens* 'Superba', *L.s.* ('Sulfurea'), virgin's bower (*Clematis flammula*), anemone clematis (*C. montana*), golden clematis (*C. tangutica*), scarlet clematis (*C. texensis*), and sweet autumn clematis (*C. paniculata*). (The bittersweet, greenbrier, and scarlet kadsura are *dioecious*, which means both

American bittersweet, grown for its bright red berries in autumn, is native to the eastern United States. To be sure of berries, plant a male plant with several female plants.

Gold flame honeysuckle got its name from its pink and yellow flowers. The buds are a bright coral color—very striking against the blue-green leaves.

Sweet autumn clematis is a billowing mass of fragrant, creamy white flowers from late summer into fall.

male and female plants must be planted to get the berries.)

Birds are especially attracted to vines on walls because of the warmth walls give off, as well as the wind protection they provide. Add a bird feeder or two and some water, and birds are virtually guaranteed all year-round. A cardinal eating red berries in the snow in one's own garden brightens a long, dark winter as nothing else can.

There is another advantage to inviting birds into your garden besides the pure pleasure of watching them. Birds eat insects. The more birds, the fewer bugs. They eat flies, mosquitoes, moths, and spiders. They also eat the scale, slugs, cutworms, and caterpillars that can infuriate even the

most benign, mildest-mannered gardener into spraying poison on everything in sight. For the thrifty, I will add that wild birds work for free. The poisons do not. It costs a lot of money, time, and effort to poison the environment to the point that insects won't live there, incidental to the very real risk to your health and that of your family, friends, and neighbors. Since most pesticides are petroleum-based, not only need there be fewer poisons on the planet, but it is another step toward reducing our dependence on foreign oil. What a lot of virtue may be purchased for the price of a few vines with berries and some birdseed! A garden that welcomes birds is prettier, easier, less expensive, and more fun.

'Climbing Blaze' is an American classic (above)
grown on fences and trellises across the country.

'Queen Elizabeth' (left) is the rose so big and
beautiful that a whole new class was created for it:
It was the first Grandiflora rose, named for Her
Majesty Queen Elizabeth II. The climbing sort is no
less superb.

THE TRULY SPECTACULAR

All the vines discussed thus far are preeminently useful. Those that follow are spectacular. These all have flowers—striking, magnificent flowers—the kind that people stop to point at, the kind that makes uninspired architecture fade into insignificance, the kind that makes dull walls a delight to the eye, the kind that turns a rather ordinary tree into an object of breathtaking beauty.

Old Garden Roses, as they are officially classified by the American Rose Society, are choice flowering vines. Not only are they spectacular in bloom, but most are naturally disease- and pest-resistant. Cabbage Roses (*Rosa centifolia*) are the lush, extravagant roses the Dutch Masters painted, each rose so big a child can bury its face in one. All are very fragrant; 'Fantin Latour' is a lovely pink, as sensuous as a Rubens nude and it grows about five feet high. One of the most beautiful white roses in the world is the damask rose (*R. damascena*) 'Madame Hardy', with huge, open, white flowers and a green eye, and like her name, she is winter hardy. 'Celsiana' is a blush pink damask that also takes cold weather well. 'York and Lancaster' is a damask rose that sometimes blooms pink, sometimes white, and sometimes, a combination of the two.

The Noisette Rose (*R. x noisettiana*) does best where late frosts don't kill it back. It has clusters of as many as one hundred fragrant roses in a single bunch, and the bush is covered with natural nosegays in spring and summer. The buds are exquisitely shaped, and full-blown the roses have that loose openness that makes one think of tea parties on the lawn at a country estate. A good one is the original cultivar, 'Champney Pink Cluster', which grows to seven feet in mild climates.

The climbing roses are also superb for breath-

Cabbage Roses (above) *are the lush, sensuous roses so often featured in the still-life paintings of the Dutch Masters.*

taking masses of roses. Some of the best are 'New Dawn', a delicate shell pink, 'Climbing Peace', a pink and yellow bicolor; 'Climbing Queen Elizabeth', pink and perfectly formed; 'City of York', a splendid white; 'Golden Showers', the best yellow; 'Blaze', a bright red, and 'Climbing Cécile Brunner', tiny and pale pink, probably better known as the baby rose or sweetheart rose.

Roses are long-lived. Some growing at Wyck in the Germantown section of Philadelphia are nearly two hundred years old. Wherever an old garden is found, no matter how overgrown and wild, the roses still remain. Roses are sturdy characters, and they all know exactly how to be roses. Most of the work surrounding roses is self-imposed: the spraying, the hard pruning, the feeding. It's a lot of work that often doesn't need to be done; in fact, I suspect the roses would do as well or better without it. Give roses a decent start—plenty of sun, good soil, and root room—keep them moist but not wet, buy disease and pest resistant varieties, provide for air circulation, then

Fragrant and lovely, 'Madame Hardy' is one of the prettiest of the old-fashioned damask roses.

stand back and let them do what they know how to do best, which is make roses. Pruning can be restricted to cutting out dead or diseased canes, spindly growth, suckers, and taking bouquets of roses to enjoy.

Vita Sackville-West inherited an old apple orchard with her Elizabethan tower at Sissinghurst, and rather than cut the trees down because they were past bearing, she grew flowering vines up them, especially clematis and roses. The apples flowered in the spring, the vines later on, giving two brilliant shows instead of one. I have recently become a convert to the practice of leaving dead trees (if whatever they died of won't infect the living ones nearby) because I suddenly realized that the fact that we seldom saw pileated woodpeckers (the big, red-cockaded "Woody the Woodpecker" woodpecker) any more

Grown up pillars as this one is, or over a garden gate or on an arbor, 'New Dawn' climbs in a cloud of pale pink.

Clematis happily climbs trees, though it may need a boost up at first. Use soft plant ties to hold them against the trunk until they're tall enough to find a twig to twine around.

For warm climates, few vines are as luxuriantly lush or as pretty as Mandevilla splendens *'Alice du Pont.'*

was because we'd assiduously and at great expense removed all the dead trees. In the future, I shall follow Sackville-West's sterling example, and think of old or dead trees as a free trellis.

Frost-free climates have a wild advantage when it comes to spectacular vines, especially if warm weather is combined with some wet weather. Bougainvillea, for starters, is a showstopper. It's the perfect complement to Mediterranean or Spanish architecture, giving even the most modest house the look of a villa. It comes in red, pink, purple, orange and white, and blooms year-round. Plant it where it doesn't have to be pruned often —it has nasty thorns.

Mandevilla splendens 'Alice du Pont' has magnificent pure pink, cup-shaped flowers and dark green, glossy leaves, and it grows typically, tropically fast.

Cup of gold (*Allamanda cathartica*) is evergreen with leathery leaves and big, soft yellow, trumpet-shaped flowers. It needs strong support because it gets very thick and heavy.

Coral vine (*Antigonon leptopus*), also known as queen's wreath, *corallita* and *rosa de montana* must, says the *Sunset New Western Garden Book*, have been loved by lots of people to have such a plethora of nice common names. It likes the hottest spot in the garden and is wonderfully drought tolerant. It climbs quickly to forty feet with dark green arrow shaped leaves and long trailing sprays of small pink flowers. Open and airy, it's the flirtatious señorita of vines, perfect for shading a patio or making a delicate tracery on a wall. In the hot weather areas where it grows best, branches of it can be twisted into a beautiful wreath for Christmas Day.

It seems a shame to restrict vines to the country when they can make the city a much nicer place to live. The tough urban conditions that discourage other plants to death merely tame the rampant vines and slow them down enough to make them well behaved. Most are easy to grow, undemanding as to maintenance, profusely floriferous, and often fragrant as well. In addition, they cheerfully screen out unattractive views, green up endless expanses of encroaching walls, absorb dirt and noise, and look pretty—what more do you want from a plant?

Cup of gold is a true tropical—best grown on a wall where it can get the warmth in which it flourishes.

CHAPTER FIVE

THE NEGLECTABLE GARDEN

T HIS IS, I AM AWARE, AN APPALLING THING for someone in the business of extolling gardening to admit, but I do not, cannot, garden all the time. Sometimes I wish I could. Other times, I'm glad I can't. I suspect, in fact, fear, that this failure is partially attributable to a lack of dexterity on my part: I have never figured out how to type with one hand and garden with the other. The remainder of this signal lack on my part is sheer laziness. I don't like a lot of what other people consider gardening.

I sometimes worry that my commitment to ecologically sound gardening has as much to do with the fact that I hate the smell and bother and work and danger of herbicides, fungicides, and pesticides as with any high-mindedness on my part. The truth is,

I'm afraid of blinding, poisoning, or giving some appalling form of cancer to myself, my family, friends, and neighbors. The truth is, I think it's a nuisance to gather up all the paraphernalia required to spray, all the special measuring cups and spoons that must never, under any circumstances, be used for anything else. The truth is, I have never been organized enough to remember what needs to be fed when and how much, much less keep a garden diary recording all this crucial information. I prefer to believe that I am politically correct, deeply moral, and sincerely concerned about the good of the planet, but I have moments of disturbing self-doubt on the subject. I may simply be lazy.

The authenticity of my ecological morality aside, even if I didn't believe that poisoning the planet is a dubious enterprise, I don't have time to do all that stuff anyway. I write a lot; I travel widely; I clean house occasionally; I eat every now and then. None of these activities is compatible with gardening.

It has been necessary to negotiate a truce between the demands of family, house, career, and the garden. Fortunately, that is fairly easy to accomplish between trees, shrubs, perennials, and bulbs. Annuals usually go by the wayside unless they self-sow, in which case they are welcomed with open arms. Garden maintenance becomes even easier by choosing plants that are native or particularly well adapted to the garden's soil and climate. Words like *self-clinging, disease-resistant, hardy, vigorous,* even *rampant* and *invasive* in catalog descriptions are music to my ears. I like the idea that the plants in my garden are inclined to cooperate with the project of making a garden. I don't want to drag them into this, kicking and screaming, or even resentful and sulking. The number of plants in my garden that must be coaxed and cajoled are few and far between. The perversity of the alpine gardener who delights in plants specifically because they are tiny and difficult and a long way from home is beyond me. That's like adopting two-year-olds only for as long as they throw temper tantrums. I prefer plants that are more like five-year-olds: easygoing, even-tempered, eager to grow up, and full of surprises.

That said, how does one go about creating the neglectable garden? One excellent way to start is to cultivate the habit of the Sunday morning stroll around the neighborhood to see what is growing enthusiastically in other people's gardens. If you don't know the names of what you see, make notes: the color, shape, and size of the flower; how it grows (flower, shrub, vine, or tree); and what the leaves look like (a hand, an oval, pointed, serrated, wavy, curled, streaked, in pairs, in threes, opposite each other or alternating, one on one side of the stem, the next on the other).

A fine way to get to know your neighbors is to ask. The question, "What's that?" accompanied by a finger pointed at a plant has started many a lifelong friendship. Once you have a name and/or a description of the intriguing and enticing creature, your next stop should be the local nursery or a nearby public garden, botanical garden, arboretum, or garden club meeting. Somebody there will probably be able to identify it.

OF HILLSIDE AND HOLLY

Perhaps this is the point at which to explain my relationship to Hillside House and Holly House. Hillside House is my city house, suburban really, in an old, established neighborhood, with neighbors on all sides. Holly is my country house in California's coastal hills, on a dirt road off a dirt road, the last house on a wooded hill surrounded by wooded hills. Hillside came with stone terraces and paths and some ancient deciduous oaks and large shrubs to work with. Holly House came

© Michael Landis

Hillside House has graciously curving flagstone paths, stone terraces, and century-old oaks.

© Michael Landis

Holly House has redwood benches built against a thirty-five-degree slope and garden paths that are not much wider than the original deer trails. 'Mount Hood' daffodils are among the many bulbs that bloom in the spring. Hostas grow magnificently, rising above the variegated silver foliage of yellow archangel.

© Michael Landis

'Loder's White' rhododendrons flourish in the filtered shade of the many oaks and madrones.

with native wilderness, a house gimbal-hung on a steep slope, some young trees, and a world of weeds. Even working with much of the same material—both gardens have rhododendrons, azaleas, and camellias, for example—they feel completely different.

At Hillside I have free rein. I study my garden books, haunt the local nurseries, arrive early at the Strybing Arboretum rare plant sale, wander around specialist nurseries, and snatch up obscure plants with cries of delight. I know exactly what needs to go where, down to the species and color. I see the garden as it will be at full maturity and am baffled by people whose vision is so limited that they can see only what is there.

At Holly, Charles, the wise and wonderful man to whom I am married, takes a more practical approach. There is a lot of land that must be planted with something and if something is to be had at an exceptionally good price from the nursery, why, he'll bring home a few dozen or more. Surely, he explains in his most reasonable voice, we can find a place for them somewhere. This nonchalant approach wreaks havoc with my elaborate garden designs and color schemes. Suddenly I find myself trying to fit purple and yellow into my summer scheme of chaste blue and white. Suddenly the long-dreamed-of hedge of English laurel that will someday frame the Mediterranean walled garden is transformed into a fifty-foot row of blue potato bush (*Lycianthus rantonnei* 'Grandiflorum'), a plant *Sunset* describes as "not easy to use in a tailored landscape." Not to mention that the deer think it's candy, fanning to flame all my fears that I do not really garden at all, but merely bait for Bambi.

Gardening by consensus does not allow for my intricately wrought plans. Better peace and harmony in the house than perfection in the garden. Both gardens are very pretty, and in no way the same, and is that not, after all, the purpose of having a city house and a country house?

© Michael Landis

© Michael Landis

Clematis lawsoniana *'Henryi'* (left) *with its ethereal white blooms clambers up the banister along with a pair of English ivies, one gray-green, the other the green and white variegated* **Hedera helix** *'Glacier'.*

At Holly House (below)*, roses bloom in pots, foxglove and rhododendrons flourish on the bank, and the hammock in the big madrone is a constant temptation, but the table on the deck is a better place for a quiet cup of tea and a book.*

Spanish bluebells are lovely, but common names are confusing when several entirely different species carry the name "bluebell."

A BRIEF DIGRESSION

At the stage of trying to identify a plant, most garden references are worse than useless; they are infuriating. Many are organized alphabetically, which assumes you already know the name of the plant. Good ones are alphabetized according to the Latin name, which you are even less likely to know than the common name. Those organized on the basis of common names are hopelessly frustrating. Spanish bluebell and English bluebell are bulbs (*Endymion hispanicus* and *E. non-scriptus*, respectively), but bluebell of Scotland is a herbaceous plant (*Campanula rotundifolia*). Knowing a poppy is a poppy is not much help. A poppy may be a California poppy (*Eschscholzia californica*), an Iceland poppy (*Papaver nudicaule*), an Oriental poppy (*P. orientale*), a Welsh poppy (*Meconopsis cambrica*), a Himalayan poppy (*M. betonicifolia*), or a Field of Flanders poppy (*P. rhoeas*), which sounds more like a lesson in geography than botany. A rose may be a rose (*Rosa* spp.), or it may be a guelder rose (*Viburnum opulus*), a Lenten rose (*Helleborus orientalus*), a rose of Sharon (*Hibiscus syriacus*), or a rosebay (*Rhododendron maximum*). Speaking of rosebay, it's completely unrelated to the bay used for cooking (*Laurus nobilis*), nor is either in any way related to the California bay (*Umbelluaria californica*). The process is a bit like looking up a word in the dictionary to find out how to spell it. If you can't spell it, you can't find it in the dictionary, and if you know how to spell it, why bother looking it up?

For reasons I find unfathomable, there are excellent field guides to native plants and trees with good keys so you can figure out what you happen to have stumbled across, but to my knowledge there's nothing of the sort available for the gardener. There is one book that attempts to solve the problem with color photographs, *What Flower Is That?* by Stirling Maccoby. Unfortunately, the emphasis is largely on tropical and subtropical plants, which limits its use in North America. Perhaps the most useful book currently available for identification of ornamentals is *The National Arboretum Book of Outstanding Garden Plants* by Jacqueline Hériteau, which is organized by growth habit: flowers, ground covers, vines, shrubs, trees, etc., and has lots of helpful photographs. It lists both common and Latin names in the index, which is a great help, and serves the Northeast, the Midwest, the Southeast, and the South very well. It also has a pronunciation guide for Latin names, which is a blessing for those whose years at school didn't happen to include Latin. For western gardeners (West Coast, Pacific Northwest, Far West, and Southwest), *The New Sunset Western Garden Book* is indispensable, but for identification it is not as useful as one might hope. It does cross-

A rose is a rose, unless it's a Lenten rose like this **Helleborus orientalus.**

reference most common names, but has line drawings rather than photographs, and not nearly enough even of those.

BACK TO THE NEGLECTABLE GARDEN

The reason for looking at other people's gardens is to learn what thrives in your neighborhood and what doesn't, not to duplicate your neighbor's garden. If, for example, the firethorn next door is covered with white mealybug and black honeydew, take the hint: don't plant a firethorn. If the pear trees in the neighborhood are afflicted with fire blight, take a miss on planting a pear tree. Choose the plants that are flourishing: They are your best bets for being well adapted to the climate and soil. They are also the best bets for not being what Marc Cathey, Director of the National Arboretum in Washington, D.C., calls "chemically dependent."

It's worthwhile noticing whether the plants are in sun or shade, since shade-lovers such as ferns and impatiens will broil in full sun and sun-lovers such as daisies (*Chrysanthemum* spp.) and geraniums (*Pelargonium* spp.) will get leggy and tatty in deep shade. Most garden books and good garden catalogs will state specifically whether a given plant does best in sun or shade, and some will even tell you how many hours of sun the plant requires.

Choose What's Choice

There is a subtext here, a subtle plot against the ordinary. Exploring other gardens allows one to create a garden of plants that are choice, a display of best of breed, if you will. Too often gardeners feel restricted to planting only those plants

available at the local garden center, which are not necessarily the most interesting, the best adapted, or the most attractive plants that could be grown. They are generally whatever is the least expensive seed for the grower to purchase, easiest for the grower to grow, taking the least time from planting to marketability, best able to stand up to the rigors of shipping, and for which there is a demonstrated market. More people buy marigolds (*Tagetas*) than hellebores (*Helleborus*) ergo more nurseries offer more choices of marigolds in greater quantities than they do the elegant Christmas rose.

Lilies have always been choice selections for the garden, and the proliferation of disease-resistant hybrids have made them even more desirable. These Mid-Century hybrids grow well in almost any soil.

A well-grown rhododendron is a dramatic addition to the spring landscape.

Weekends spent wandering around public gardens in your area are pleasant and highly informative. Specialist nurseries can be illuminating in their range of wonderful things you've never seen before: geraniums with flowers like big azaleas, blue rhododendrons, roses that date from colonial times, native plants so striking you understand why even today English gardens achieve their lovely effects with plants native to North America, everything from redwoods (*Sequoia sempervirens*) to California lilac (*Ceanothus* spp.) to wandering Jew.

A brief aside: One day in London I decided to seek out the small churchyard where two of England's most famous plant collectors are buried, the John Tradescants, father and son. In renovating the churchyard garden, someone hit upon the inspired idea of using plants the Tradescants Elder and Younger had found in their explorations. John Tradescant the Younger (1608–1662) is generally credited as the first European gardener and botanist to go a-hunting for plants in North America. He made three trips to the Virginia colony in his capacity as royal gardener, fetching home to En-

The brilliant colors of autumn are a treat to look forward to with a red maple like this one.

The tulip tree is a North American native first collected by the Royal Gardener, John Tradescant the Younger, in the seventeenth century.

gland such sparkling botanical jewels as the red maple (*Acer rubrum*), the tulip tree (*Liriodendron tulipfera*), virginia creeper, and Michaelmas daisies (*Aster novi-angliae*). To wander in the little church-yard garden filled with flowers from North America was like unexpectedly finding friends from home on that damp, gray day in London.

Going to botanical gardens, arboretums, and plant society fund-raising sales broadens the selection substantially, and often at lower prices than commercial garden centers. There is also a world of information to be had. Knowledgeable horticulturists, long-experienced gardeners, and expert amateurs tend to frequent such places. From a man whose name I never learned I discovered that the 'Loder's White' rhododendron is really not a Loder's, despite its name, and that 'King George', a huge and magnificent white rhododendron, is. (The Loder's rhododendrons [*R.* x *loderi*], a cross

between *R. fortunei* and *R. griffithianum* (1901) are considered to be among the finest of the hybrid rhododendrons.)

At a daffodil society show, I found out that a clump of daffodils I'd snatched from the path of a road-widening bulldozer were a type now no longer available. A geranium society show demonstrated clearly that it was time to stop loathing geraniums and to learn to love them as pelargoniums instead. The zonal geraniums (*Pelargonium hortorum*) are still not welcome in my garden, but the Regal geraniums (*P. domesticum*) have found a happy home in a hot, sunny corner, and are blooming beautifully with large azalea-shaped flowers in pale pink and white. One of the fascinating things about gardening is that there is always more to learn, always a lovely new plant to meet, always something teasing and tugging one a little further down the garden path.

'King George', a superb turn-of-the-century hybrid rhododendron, takes ten years to come to bloom, and is worth the wait.

MEANWHILE, BACK AT THE GARDEN

Gardens must be built from the ground up, but they must be organized from the top down. The most significant living structures in the garden are the trees, simply because their size influences everything from wind patterns to temperature to soil acidity to what will grow under them. Trees and large shrubs are the skeleton of the garden, giving it shape and form; flowers and ground covers fill it in and flesh it out.

The primary key to the neglectable garden is: Plant it once. This encompasses trees, shrubs, vines, ground covers, and perennial flowers. Annuals, which must be planted and pulled and replanted each season, have little place in the neglectable garden. Once planted, gardens, like children, do best with a bit of benign neglect. Just as children need time to daydream and wool-gather, plants don't do well if fussed over too much. Overfed plants, like overfed children, are neither healthy nor happy. Essentially, plants come knowing how to grow and bloom, just as children do. Given basic care and a modicum of loving attention, both do just fine.

The second key is to tilt the odds in the gardens' favor by choosing plants that are naturally inclined to do well in your area. That's what the Sunday morning constitutional and weekend afternoons at the plant society sale are all about. Choose the best-adapted, choicest plants you can find, give them an appropriate spot and adequate space, and get out of their way.

If this all sounds terribly vague and theoretical, let me ground it with some examples. The garden I am working on now is recently wrested from wilderness. It is a mixed California live oak, bay, and madrone (*Arbutus menziesii*) woodland, most of it on a thirty-five degree slope with heavy clay soil. Since the trees were already there, it was largely a matter of selecting which ones would stay. The bays, being broadleaf evergreens, created deep, dark shade and its leaves made the soil very acid, both of which severely restricted anything from growing under them. They were cut to about a foot high and allowed to come back as handsome, bushy shrubs. In addition, the native toyons (California holly, Christmas berry, specifically *Heteromeles arbutifolia*) were retained, though like the bays they were cut to the ground to come back as fine dense shrubs instead of the thin, scraggly little trees of their previous incarnation. The oaks, which are evergreen, were called "holly leaf oak" by the early explorers because their dark green, prickly leaves are reminiscent of English holly in both their shape and their spines. As California's native oaks are disappearing rapidly under the threat of development, all the healthy oaks were saved. The steeply sloped location is important here because coast live oaks are adapted to long periods of drought—in Northern California, nine months of the year without rain is typical, accompanied by three months of heavy rains. The steep slope makes the rain drain off quickly, so the trees are never standing in water, despite the heavy soil. Native oaks do poorly in lawns and most gardens —regular watering rots the roots out.

The madrone is a choice tree, not often grown successfully outside its native haunts. (It is demanding in its requirements and does not transplant well.) In addition to being rare, it is striking. I quote its description from *The Trees Around Us* by Barber and Phillips: "Its vivid cinnamon-red or tawny orange bark, its burnished leaves, ice-blue on the reverse, and its erect pyramids of white flowers in April, followed in summer by fruits that vary from orange to crimson, make it a stunning spectacle, the essence of elegant strength." The flowers look very much like lily-of-the-valley and attract hummingbirds; the fruits attract a

California holly is the shrub that gave Holly House its name. It is also called toyon and Christmas berry.

Azaleas planted in sweeping drifts give the dramatic effect of massing without the artificial note that's struck by closely planted formal beds.

number of seed-eating birds, particularly the bright blue Steller's jay. *The New Sunset Western Garden Book* says bluntly, "If you live in madrone country and have a tree in your garden, treasure it." *Sunset* please note: All twenty-seven madrones and thirty-two coast live oaks in my garden are duly treasured. (I forgot to count the toyons, but it's something over a dozen.)

Most of the trees in this garden are quite young, few older than fifty years. They are perfectly capable of living another two hundred years or more. The real point of that observation is that they will one day be substantially larger than they are right now. The live oaks at Descanso Gardens in Glendale, California (which has the largest collection of camellias [*Camellia*] in the United States), are already more than a century old and provide a high and lovely dappled shade for the gardens. Taking my own advice of borrowing ideas from other, older gardens, the major shrubs of my garden are camellias, rhododendrons, and azaleas. Camellias and rhododendrons are also long-lived plants capable of breaking the century mark. I daydream about what this flowering woodland will look like a hundred years from now when the rhododendrons have grown to thirty feet or more, and the camellias are twenty feet high and as wide, the trees seventy-five to one hundred feet tall, with "pools and puddles" of sunlight (to borrow Nabakov's description), dappling green leaves, and dark ground.

Another goal at Holly House—named for the California holly—is to have color or bloom in the garden every day of the year. The camellias begin blooming in October and different bushes keep the bloom going all through winter into May, though the majority bloom from January to March. One royal purple rhododendron blooms every year in October and again late in the spring. A single white azalea does the same. In the sunny garden, the cosmos (*Cosmos*) and petunias (*Petunia*)

Lady's eardrops, or Gartenmeister fuchsias, are an old-fashioned shrub fuchsia that grows especially well at Holly House, blooming from summer through fall.

produce one last glorious burst in late October. White impatiens left over from last summer continue to bloom through the fall until the cold kills them; given a protected spot or no frost, they will soldier on all through the winter. The same is true of hanging baskets of pink impatiens. White Japanese anemone (*Anemone* x *hybrida*) bloom from August through October, along with the fuchsias and monkshood. The paperbark maple colors crimson. In November, the nandina, wild honeysuckle (*Lonicera hispidula*), and toyon are bright with red berries as befits the coming of the holidays, and the cyclamen (*Cyclamen*) are putting up their red-tinged leaves and buds.

There is a fine collection of maples scattered throughout this garden: in the woodland are three clumps of Japanese maples, a native big-leaf maple, and a paperbark maple. All turn red in the fall except the big-leaf maple, which is an exclamation point of yellow. There is another clump of Japanese maples on the opposite side of the house, a red maple, two snakebark maples (*A. grosseri* 'Hersii'), and two specimen Japanese maples, one a magnificent laceleaf maple (*A. palmatum* 'Dissectum atropurpureum'), the other a vigorous, fifteen-foot Japanese maple (*A.p.* 'Heptalobum Osakazuki') with green leaves that turn fiery scarlet. The Japanese maples in a cobalt blue bonzai pot brings the collection to a total of twenty-one trees.

The camellias and cyclamen (*Cyclamen persicum*) bloom in December and January. By February the earliest bulbs are blooming, the jonquils (*Narcissus jonquilla*), narcissus, and grape hyacinth (*Muscari armeniacum*) first, followed by daffodils, and tulips. In March and April the rhododendrons, azaleas, weigela, sweet mock orange, white lilac, foxglove (*Digitalis*), and fuchsias (*Fuchsia*) put on the big show, in blazing red and white. Late spring sees the return of the plantain lilies (*Hosta* spp.) grown mostly for their lovely leaves, wisteria, poor man's rhododendron (*Impatiens oliveri*), Mexican evening primrose (*Oenothera berlandieri*), and escallonia (*Escallonia*), flowering in pinks and pale lavenders that carry the garden color scheme gently from spring's bright red and white into the summer's blue and white. The summer lilies, star jasmine, Chilean jasmine, delphinium, canterbury-bells (*Campanula medium*), rover bluebell (*C. rapunculoides*), Spanish bluebell, allium, blue camassia (*Camassia*), blue and white poppy-flowered anemones (*Anemone coronaria* Monarch de Caen 'Blue Poppy' and 'The Bride'), blue balloon flower (*Platycoodon grandiflorus*), Chinese ground orchid (*Bletilla striata 'Alba'*), maiden's wreath (*Francoa*), meadowsweet, and white coral bells (*Heuchera richardsonii*) carry the summer garden from May through October in shades of blues and white.

The hummingbird garden, consisting of madrone blossoms, fuchsias, weigela, escallonia, coral bells, red valerian (*Centranthus ruber*), sticky monkey flower (*Mimnulus aurantiaus*), wild honeysuckle, and a dozen beard tongues (*Penstemon* spp.) in various shades from red to pink to white, has one thing or another in bloom pretty much year-round to appease the amazing appetites of the Anna's hummingbirds that are resident here.

The wildflowers that have volunteered have been welcomed warmly. Grass iris (*Iris douglasiana*), blue-eyed grass (*Sisyrinchium bellum*), rein orchids (*Habenaria* spp.), coralroot orchids (*Corallorhiza striata*), sticky monkey flower, and wild honeysuckle are all received with enthusiasm. Only the Scotch broom, poison oak, and blackberry are strictly forbidden entrance.

Fragrance is also a large part of the pleasure of Holly House. In the spring the Chinese sacred lilies and daffodils smell deliciously; come summer, star jasmine scents the air. Later, the Chilean jasmine vine sweetens the entry. Several Maddenii rhododendrons (*Rhododendron Maddenii*) were purchased primarily because their fragrance was described as "chocolate-cinnamon," and if it's true, I shall have to be forcibly dragged away from them when they're in bloom. Another delightful

© Michael Landis

The new foliage of lily-of-the-valley shrub (Pieris japonica *'Mountain Flame') very nearly overshadows the flowers with its brilliance.*

Calla lilies have been hybridized in a wide range of colors and sizes, and the smaller ones are now sold as houseplants.

surprise was a rhododendron with richly aromatic foliage; sometimes I rub the leaves just to get the fragrance on my hands. The bay trees also have strongly scented leaves that make the air fragrant after the rain, and the true bay, a potted Grecian laurel, does the same by the front door. In the sunny garden, three 'Queen Elizabeth' roses add their fragrance planted just off the deck. (The one concession this house has made to the California style of landscaping is that it has decks everywhere. Of five doors that open to the outside, only one does not open onto a deck, and when the master plan is completed, it will as well.)

One small section at the bottom of the garden is perpetually damp. It was officially declared the bog garden and a patriotic combination of red, white, and blue—calla lilies, cardinal flower, and western blue flag (*Iris missouriensis*)—is planted. To set these off, leopard plant (*Ligularia tussilaginea*

'Aureo-maculata') was added for its yellow-speckled leaves, bear's breech (*Acanthus mollis*) for its big, shining dark green leaves, and variegated spider plant (*Chlorophytum comosum*) for its white-striped leaves. They all like what amounts to mud, so a pipe now feeds the used water from the shower into the bog to prevent any chance of its drying out during the summer months. Since it is said that God began with a garden, is this what's meant by cleanliness being next to godliness?

There are a number of plants that flourish at Holly House that are generally considered house plants in colder climates. The spider plant is one of them; it works here as a clumping ground cover. Another is false sea onion (*Ornithogalum caudatum*), pots of which are massed on the front deck. I am never quite sure how to classify the *Cymbidium* orchids, whether as garden plants or houseplants. I do not have them planted out in the garden, though I know of a house not far from mine where they are. Neither do they spend the winter inside, exactly. These are in pots on shelves that hang off the front deck. Being cool-growing orchids they will take temperatures below freezing, though not for more than eight hours. They are brought inside only when they bloom and they often remain in bloom for two or three months. When the last bud blooms, they go back outdoors. With approximately one hundred pots of *Cymbidiums*, we have orchids blooming in the house ten months of the year, from October to July.

ON THE SUBJECT OF NEGLECT

All of the plants that I've described meet the criteria of being neglectable: They can be planted once and left to grow on their own, which they do quite happily. Water is supplied by a conscientiously water conservative drip-trickle system: Each plant gets its sprayer when it's planted. None require either fertilizing or regular pruning. In fact, the most demanding garden chore in this garden is raking the paths. Even then the leaves are dumped unceremoniously into a pile we dignify beyond all knowing with the name of compost heap. When the fireplace gets full, we add the wood ashes, water it in, and every year it produces perfectly lovely soil. We never turn it, add nitrogen, manure, or anything else to it.

The birds pretty well take care of any insect pests, and we do provide food and water for the birds. It seems the smallest sort of thanks we can give them for not having to spray. Shouting and throwing pebbles to rattle the leaves and making a lot of noise scares off the cats and the deer, but I'm not sure that counts as a garden chore. Mostly, we plant. Charles says pretty soon there will be no place I can put a trowel that doesn't have something else already planted there, but I don't think that's true. Surely, as he always tells me, we can find a place for it somewhere.

Woodland gardens in spring with flowering dogwood and azaleas in bloom have a haunting charm, a special sense of peace too seldom found in one's daily round.

CHAPTER SIX

THE COTTAGE GARDEN

COTTAGE GARDENS OF EIGHTEENTH- AND nineteenth-century England grew out of harsh imperatives: the need to grow vegetables for food and herbs for medicine in a very small space. Cottagers did not have fields of their own to till; they tilled the fields of the landed gentry and the aristocracy to whom the crops belonged. They did not avail themselves of doctors; medicine was the province of women who doctored their own families with the herbs they grew. They had but little space in which to grow what they needed, often no more than a dooryard. Plants were crammed in together, cabbages with Madonna lilies, (*Lilium candidum*) parsley with pot marigold (*Calendula*), apples with foxglove. Cabbage provided food through the winter, foxglove is yet today the basis for the powerful heart medicine digitalis, parsley flavored food otherwise not especially flavorful, pot marigold brightened soups and salads with its petals and also made a bright yellow dye, apples kept the doctor away, and lilies kept the wolf from the door. Literally.

The Goodman of Paris (*Le Menagier de Paris*, c. 1393) recommended this recipe to kill wolves: "Take the root of the black hellebore (it is the hellebore that hath the white flower) and dry the root thoroughly and not in the sun, and clean the earth therefrom; and then make it into powder in a mortar and with this powder mix a fifth part of glass well ground and a fourth part of lily leaf, and let it all be mixed and pounded together so that it can be passed through a sieve...take honey and fresh fat in equal part and mix them with the aforesaid powder, and make it into a hard and stiff paste, rolling it into round balls the size of a hen's egg, and cover the aforesaid balls with fresh fat and lay them upon stones and shards in the places where...wolves and foxes will come."

To kill rats, the recipe was far simpler: "cakes of paste and cheese and powdered aconite [monkshood]" set near their holes "where they have naught to drink."

Flowers like monkshood, foxglove, roses, and lilies were grown in the cottage garden for their practical uses; beauty was incidental. But their beauty cannot be denied, and it was Gertrude Jekyll who transformed this practical, edible landscape into a purely ornamental effect. She rescued the honest, old-fashioned flowers of the cottagers, long ignored in the gardens of the wealthy, and made them the basis for her famous borders.

The great gardens of the gentry and nobility had preferred to feature the rare, exotic species from North America, collected by the English Tradescants, father and son, the American Quakers, John and William Bartram, also father and son, and that redoubtable Scot, David Douglas, who sent back such a proliferation of West Coast trees that he wrote William Jackson Hooker, the Director at Kew, "you will begin to think that I manufacture pines at my pleasure." (Not everyone approved of the passion for installing American plants in English gardens. Sir William Chambers wrote in 1772, "...the ax has often, in one day, laid waste the growth of several ages; and thousands of venerable plants, whole woods of them, have been swept away, to make room for a little grass, and a few American weeds.")

There is something very odd, and very droll in the fact that the current passion for English gardens in North America consists to a remarkable extent of bringing our own species back home, almost as though we could not see the magnificence of our native trees and flowers until the British took them from the forests and prairies and placed them in a garden setting. Gertude Jekyll's great contribution was to see the ornamental in the purely practical, anticipating by many years the dictum that form follows function.

THE PRACTICAL GARDEN

It has become fashionable recently to speak of the edible landscape, as though growing vegetables with flowers is wildly daring. And indeed, when the phrase first began to be used, it was. Vegetables were treated like the pariahs of the plant world. We behaved as though the vegetable plot were a conspiracy to undermine the government. Vegetables were banished to the farthest reaches of the backyard, regimented into rows, bound to stakes, confined to cages, and otherwise treated like dangerous malcontents. They were expected to produce, and otherwise stay out of sight.

Yet even under these conditions, there was great beauty in the vegetable ghetto. Hired to teach biodynamic organic gardening at the local college,

I was given a plot in the middle of the campus. Since the college was built on what had been the grounds of a great country estate, handsomely landscaped, the vegetable garden seemed painfully obtrusive, dreadfully exposed, indeed, embarrassingly naked, in the midst of those vast lawns and mighty trees. The students got a lesson in vertical gardening as I attempted to disguise or hide the garden. We grew cherry tomatoes (*Lycopersicum cerasiforne*) up one side of a chain link fence and scarlet runner beans on another, and watered them lavishly to make them lush. We blocked the view from one end with artichokes (*Cynara scolymus*), and on the other with its cousin, cardoon. We planted the corners with rhubarb (*Rheum rhabarbarum*), and manured it heavily to get enormous leaves and massive flowers. We designed the red and green chards into intricate patterns, and made a knot garden with the herbs. We edged the tomato beds with tall African marigolds (*Tagetes erecta*) and the lettuce beds with short, neat French marigolds (*T. patula*), as though we were going to pass them off as proper flower beds. You'd have thought we were doing something unspeakable, growing vegetables *in public*.

The tradition of the cottage garden had already demonstrated that there is no reason not to grow flowers and vegetables together, and in fact, there are quite a few good reasons why they should be. Companion planting is one of the best. Some plants help other plants grow better. Marigolds kill nematodes in the soil and keep off whitefly. They should always be grown with tomatoes and potatoes. Mister-John-Henry (*T. minuta*) is even more effective (read: even more pungent, for it is the smell that keeps the bugs away) than the French marigold or the African marigold. Heaven alone knows why the French marigold is called French when it's native to Mexico, but I suspect that the Indian women who worked the soil recognized its power, for the marigold was sacred

African marigolds are excellent companion plants. The slightly bitter fragrance seems to be the key in discouraging pests.

to the goddess of agriculture in ancient Mexico. Since tomatoes and potatoes are also native to Central and South America, the solution existed side-by-side with the need.

Foxglove (*Digitalis purpurea*) stimulates growth and increases the disease resistance of whatever grows close to it; fava beans (*Vicia faba*) and clover (*Trifolium*) increase nitrogen in the soil, which makes nearby plants grow bigger and healthier; parsley makes roses more fragrant; borage is good for strawberries; and nasturtiums discourage aphids and whitefly. Garlic (*Allium sativum*) planted next to roses keeps greenfly away; indeed, a garden planted enthusiastically with leeks (*A. ampeloprasum*), onions (*A. cepa*), chives, and garlic (all members of the *Allium* family) can pretty well forget about insect pests. The *Allium* are also dramatically decorative, if you'd just as soon have flowers as eat the bulbs. (Remember, once they've bloomed, they're no longer edible.) Rhubarb stems buried near cabbage prevents clubroot, and sage, mint (*Mentha* spp.), thyme, and rosemary all help keep off the myriad of munching critters that plague cabbage.

Another good reason to plant flowers, herbs, fruits, and vegetables together is to have a supply of fresh, organically grown fruits and vegetables seasonally ready at hand. Vegetables sold in markets are sold by the pound: the bigger the vegetable, the more the farmer is paid for it. Unfortunately, many vegetables lose both flavor and texture as they get larger. When the demand hit for baby vegetables a few years ago, the consumer's attempt to find flavor and texture again, they cost a small fortune, almost as much per ounce as their larger cousins did per pound. The solution to the madness of buying vegetables so tasteless and tough that nobody wants to eat them or so expensive that baby zucchini (*Cucurbita pepo* var. *Melopepo zucchini*) and carrots (*Daucus carota* var. *Sativus*) are the price of gold futures, is simple: grow your own.

In the cottage garden, carrots make a lovely edging, their tops as prettily delicate as ferns. I grow asparagus in a terrace with daffodils and summer lilies. The spears are picked faithfully in the spring while the daffodils are blooming, and in the summer, allowed to grow into a feathery, dark green background to set off the lilies. Strawberries make a good ground cover and an equally effective edging. Curled parsley and sweet alyssum nestle neatly around garden benches, and parsley and bright yellow pansies are charming together.

For nearly two hundred years after their introduction to Europe, tomatoes were called love apples and grown exclusively as ornamentals in both England and North America, because they were popularly believed to be poisonous. Today small red peppers (*Capsicum annuum*) are sold as ornamental houseplants at Christmas. Artichokes

and cardoon are striking architectural plants with dramatic, silver-gray leaves. Rhubarb's red stems combined with red chard make even the dullest corner interesting. Grow grapes over an arbor or a gazebo or have a hedge of blueberries. Think of a fence as an opportunity to grow raspberries (*Rubus idaeus*), tomatoes, beans, peas, and cucumbers (*Cucumis sativus*); a stone or brick wall, a chance to espalier peaches and apricots.

Another small college near here, run by nuns of the Dominican Order, is also built on an old estate. The garden was originally planted with fruit trees everywhere, and the banks of the stream that runs through the grounds are covered with wild blackberry brambles. An old grape arbor runs along one side of the cutting garden. With all the peaches, apricots, nectarines (*Prunus persica* var. *nucipersica*), plums, apples, pears, cherries, grapes, blackberries, and raspberries, it is perfectly possible to eat one's way around the campus.

It is one of the odd truths that we see only what we are looking for, that things are whatever we expect them to be. A well-known study found that when teachers were told that a group of children of low intelligence were brilliant, the teachers taught as if the children were brilliant, and the children responded brilliantly. If we look at fruits and vegetables as attractive plants that just happen to also be edible, they fit beautifully into the ornamental garden in a remarkable number of ways.

THE POETIC GARDEN

Perhaps one of the most delightful parts of planning a cottage garden is the wondrously evocative names of the old-fashioned flowers. What romantic notions are evoked by love-in-a-mist (*Nigella damascena*), what anguish by love-lies-bleeding (*Amaranthus caudatus*), what sweet sadness by forget-me-not (*Myosotis sylvatica*), what happiness

Bleeding heart is one of the old-fashioned cottage garden flowers with a richly evocative name to match its curious flowers and fernlike leaves.

Johnny-jump-ups have a jaunty name to match their cheerful faces in the garden. They have a lovely tendency to reseed and come back year after year.

by heart's-ease (*Viola* x *wittrockiana*). Cupid's-dart (*Catananche caerulea*) and bleeding-heart (*Dicentra spectabilis*), bachelor's-button (*Centaurea cyanus*) and lady's-mantle (*Alchemilla*), fleur-de-lis (*Iris* x *germanica*) and lords-and-ladies (*Arum maculatum*), scarlet pimpernel (*Anagallis arvensis*) and golden Marguerite (*Chrysanthemum frutescens*), columbine (*Aquilegia*) and eglantine (*Rosa eglanteria*), woodbine (*Clematis virginiana*) and woad (*Isatis*), foxglove and wolfsbane (*Aconitum lycoctonum*), monkshood and deadly nightshade (*Solanum dulcamara*), Johnny-jump-up (*Viola pedunculata*) and trout lily (*Erythronium americanum*), honesty (*Lunaria annua*) and thrift (*Armeria*)—I don't even have to know what they look like to want them in the garden. They remind me of Edna St.

Vincent Millay's "Counting Out Rhyme" done with the names of American trees.

That's what I want even before I even get started on the antique roses. The cabbage rose 'Fantin Latour'; the moss rose 'Gloire de Mousseuses'; the China rose 'Mutabilis' that changes from pink to orange-yellow; the Bourbon rose 'La Reine Victoria'; the white rose of York 'Celestial', the yellow rose of Texas, Harison's Yellow; the apothecary rose, Rosa Mundi, which dates from 1581; the sweetbrier or eglantine, with leaves that smell like pippins; the *Rosa rugosa* 'Blanc Double de Coubert'; the tea roses brought all the way from China in the 1700's—I want all of these, too.

The very names take me back in time and space, to medieval cloister gardens, to colonial gardens,

There is no single tree more evocative of pastoral peace and pleasure than the apple tree. Mies van der Rohe notwithstanding, with apple trees, more is better.

to pioneer gardens. My mind strays to the exotic places from which these trees and flowers came: the American forests that stretched from the East Coast to the Great Plains, the high Andes and the South American rain forests, the cool streamsides and the searing deserts. I get a catch in my throat when I think of the carefully cut slips lurched along in Conestoga wagons to new, unknown, and lonely lands; of seeds and bulbs cherished through long voyages across the sea and brought home by sailors from the Cape of Good Hope; of all the combinations gardens are of the familiar and the faraway.

FRUIT IN THE COTTAGE GARDEN

The original cottagers grew fruit in their dooryard garden because orchards, like fields and forests, belonged to the lord of the manor. Apples were particularly prized: They were good fresh, kept

Periwinkle (Vinca minor) *is an extremely tough ground cover, excellent for erosion control and drought-resistant, too.*

well, and were easily preserved by drying, besides the pleasures of apple juice and cider.

Today there are so many possibilities. There is so much more to apples than the standard supermarket Red Delicious. Consider a dwarf apple, which grows to only eight feet tall, perfect for tiny urban gardens or potted on a balcony. Or the semidwarf which goes to ten or twelve feet tall. Or standards which are about twenty feet tall.

Consider heirloom apples, the kinds that are no longer available in markets: Cox's Orange Pippin, the Macintosh 'Liberty', Stayman Winesap, White Pearmain, Calville Blanc, Spitzenberg, or Rosebrook Gravenstein, to name but a few.

Any fruit tree offers not only summer fruit, but spring bloom as well. Evanescent in the garden, whether apple blossoms or cherry blossoms, this is the essence of spring, the brightest symbol of the season, the ultimate proof that winter passes.

THE URBAN COTTAGE GARDEN

How much prettier our cities could be if the miniscule front yards of town houses and brownstones were planted as cottage gardens. Given a brownstone, I would plant a pair of matching apple trees to be the heralds of spring in the middle of each half of the yard. Along the front I'd put in a one-foot-wide bed dense with yellow daffodils coming up through bird's-foot ivy, (*Hedera helix* 'Pedata') that twined itself up the posts of a three-foot wrought-iron fence that surrounded the garden. Under the apple trees, a small wooden bench encircling the trunk or a pair of old-fashioned cast-iron chairs painted white on a patch of grass or periwinkle (*Vinca minor*). Boston ivy would grow up the walls of the house itself, and in front of the house, white spires of foxtail lily (*Eremurus*), clumps of massive larkspur, monks-

A bed of bearded iris makes a grand show in the spring and the gray-green sword-shaped leaves are handsome as well. Iris don't require a lot of space to make an effective display.

hood, old-fashioned tall hollyhocks (*Alcea*), a few antique shrub roses, day lilies, cardinal flower, Canterbury-bells, tall bearded iris, Madonna lilies, Japanese anemones, meadowsweet, and last of all, columbine.

These are listed pretty much by height, from tallest to smallest. As in a border, the tallest flowers need to be in the back, the medium-sized plants in the middle ground, the shortest in front. The foxtail lily, larkspur, monkshood, and hollyhocks all grow from six to nine feet; the shrub roses, cardinal flower, and cosmos, from four to six feet; the Canterbury-bells, tall bearded iris, Japanese

anemones, and Madonna lilies, from two to four feet; and the meadowsweet and columbine from one to two and a half feet tall. Like a border, cottage gardens look best crammed with flowers.

At the far corners of the house, one at each end, I'd plant a pair of lilacs or sweet mock orange for their fragrance. "Are there lilac trees in the heart of town?/Can you hear a lark in any other part of town?..." I can't guarantee that a garden such as this will cause eager lovers to serenade on the sidewalk outside your door, but such things have been said to happen.

A neat, low holly hedge, would line the path to

Cardinal flower is a striking American native that loves a boggy place. It has the finest red of any flower that grows.

the house, and the path would be of herringbone brick. On the opposite fence lines, I'd plant a long row of asparagus. Asparagus beds can live nearly a hundred years, so it is important to prepare them well at the start. Dig a trench a foot wide and eight inches deep and fill it half full with compost and well-rotted manure. (Well-rotted manure sounds positively bizarre, I know, especially to city dwellers, but any riding stable can supply it, and most are delighted to have you haul it away. Well-rotted makes it sound as though it should smell awful, but that is merely the perversity of terminology. Fresh manure smells awful, well-rotted doesn't smell at all. Bring your own leaf bags and a shovel, and go to it.) Soak the compost and manure in the trench. Lay roots no smaller than

a man's hand (two- or three-year-old roots) twelve inches apart, cover them with two inches of soil, and water again. This leaves a trench about two inches deep, which is filled in with soil as the spears grow.

The first year, don't harvest; the purpose is to grow strong roots. The second year, cut spears for no more than a month or six weeks. When you eat asparagus, you're eating immature leaves. The third year, harvest for eight to ten weeks. After the harvest, let the tall, graceful, feathery, leaves grow; they are ornamental in the grand manner.

In all the little nooks and crannies in between the flowers I'd tuck parsley, lettuces, carrots, chard, beets, and radishes (*Raphanus sativus*) or *fraises de bois* (alpine strawberries). At the steps to the front door, I'd place two formal pots of arborvitae or bay

Fresh asparagus is a pleasure to eat and a pleasure to look at. The mature leaves make a delicate, airy background for flowers.

115

laurel; at the door itself, a pot of white busy Lizzy (*Impatiens wallerana*), and upon the door, a welcoming wreath.

All of these plants are perennials with the exception of the Canterbury-bells, a biennial. Most of the vegetables function as annuals, except the asparagus and alpine strawberries. The arborvitae falls into the category of a cast-iron plant; it grows almost no matter what. The vast majority of the plants in the garden are so hardy and adaptable that this garden could be grown pretty much anywhere. Such a garden would not take a great deal of time or money, yet it would delight the souls of those lucky enough to read the Sunday paper on the benches beneath its trees, and would enchant the eye of all who happened to pass by.

ON THE TOPIC OF TREES

Even more than architecture, trees give a place its sense of place. I chose apple trees for the urban cottage garden because apple trees symbolize the country, the rural, the pastoral, more effectively than any other tree. The flourish of apple blossoms in the spring, the quiet shade in the summer, the abundance of crisp fruit in the fall, the strong, weathered bare branches of winter, all speak eloquently of the American countryside.

By the same token, jacaranda (*Jacaranda mimosifolia*) bespeaks a warmer climate. They line the broad avenues of la Zona Rosa in Mexico City, and when the exquisite blue flowers fall, they cover the sidewalks in a blanket of blue. In Berlin before the war, the linden (*Tilia*) formed handsome allées, the trees overarching streets and cosmopolitan cafés in a cool tunnel of dappled shade. In Provence, Lombardy poplars (*Populus nigra* 'Italica') stand at attention along the roads, spires of clear yellow in the fall. In southern Italy, the drives to

great villas are typically lined with dark cypress (*Cupressus sempervirens*). In London, near Holland Park, the streets are planted on either side with the London plane (*Platanus* x *acerifolia*).

The trees define the sense of place, and eventually, come to symbolize it. Can you imagine Japan without cherry blossoms, Chinese gardens without weeping willows (*Salix babylonica*), New England without maples, the South without magnolias (*Magnolia grandiflora*), California without redwoods? When we plant trees in our gardens, they bring these associations with them, bag and baggage. Just as the Japanese suggest a stream with a meandering course of rounded pebbles, we suggest the country and all it implies of simplicity and peace when we plant an apple tree in the city.

The splendid boughs of the London plane* (Platanus x accrifolia) *filter the light like the trees near Holland Park in London.

Weeping willows are a lovely and graceful tree, but they need lots of water and lots of room. I used to play under one that had all the branches trimmed out except the outermost ones, which swept the ground like a curtain on all sides, making a cool, green summer playhouse.

THE CAST-IRON PLANTS

Cottage gardens were not grown for recreational purposes. The cottagers who grew them did not have leisure time, as we define it in this century. The plants they grew tended to be sturdy characters, capable of growing and thriving without a lot of time-consuming coddling. They fall into the category I call cast-iron plants: For the most part they can be planted, and they'll take care of themselves with no further fussing.

Every region has some of these cast-iron plants. They do need soil, though often not particularly good soil. They do need water, though often not much water. Once planted in the garden, they are

there until the bulldozers come. If they are annuals or biennials, they self-sow. They make growing a cottage garden far easier than those intimidating diagrams I see in garden magazines with little colored circles neatly laid out, seeds that must be started on the windowsill three months before they can be set out, with plants that are native to bogs cheek-by-jowl with plants that require summer dormancy and will tolerate no water whatever six months of the year.

Flowers that grow well left pretty much to their own devices are daylilies (*Hemerocallis*), daffodils, giant snowdrop (*Galanthus elwesii*), Spanish bluebell, Siberian squill (*Scilla siberica*), bearded iris, and Resurrection lily (*Lycoris squamigera*). In warm climates Belladonna lily (*Amaryllis bella-*

donna), lily-of-the-Nile (*Agapanthus africanus*), and honeysuckle, plus most of those already listed, will perform with a minimum of care. The cottage garden that uses these sturdy reliables wisely will require little beyond the basic maintenance of watering and tidying up.

Evergreen troupers in fairly cold climates include English ivy and winter creeper, both of which climb walls; American holly (*Ilex opaca*), Oregon grape (*Mahonia aquifolium*), arborvitae, juniper (*Juniperus* spp.), yew, Korean boxwood (*Buxus microphylla koreana*) for hedges; lily-of-the-valley bush (*Pieris japonica*), Purple laurel (*Rhododendron catawbiense*), Rosebay (*R. maximum*), and moun-

Airy and delicate in appearance, Tree-of-heaven is really extremely tough, eduring all hardship and bringing beauty where little was found before.

In her "Counting Out Rhyme" of American trees, Edna St. Vincent Millay wrote: "Wood of popple pale as moonbeam/Wood of oak for yoke and barn-beam/Wood of hornbeam...." I never see an American hornbeam like this one without mentally reciting her poem.

tain laurel (*Kalmia latifolia*) for shrubs. These all need shade and shelter from winter wind and sun; grow them where they are protected by walls or conifers.

Tree-of-heaven (*Ailanthus altissima*) was brought from China by the Chinese coolies imported to build the transcontinental railroad. It was grown in China in the courtyards of many temples, and the Chinese brought its seeds with them to remind themselves of home. Delicate and airy in appearance, it is tough enough to grow anywhere. This is the title tree of Betty Smith's *A Tree Grows in Brooklyn*. It looks lovely, grows rapidly to fifty feet, and suckers and reseeds prolifically. It needs trimming to keep the suckers under control and weeding to prevent it from becoming an *Ailanthus* forest, but it is the tree to grow where you honestly believe nothing will grow. Other good trees for difficult urban conditions—dirt, dust, smoke, heat, drought, poor soil, *et al*—are: male ginkgo (*Ginkgo biloba*)—the females produce foul-smelling fruit; paper mulberry (*Broussonetia papyrifera*), which is not a great tree, but like *Ailanthus*, grows where practically nothing else will; American hornbeam (*Carpinus caroliniana*), which grows everywhere, tolerates wet soil and shade, and has great fall color; red oak (*Quercus rubra*), which tolerates pollution, but needs moist, well-drained, fertile, acid soil and has magnificent wine-red leaves spring and fall; black locust (*Robinia pseudoacacia* 'Inermis'), which is thornless, very fast growing, has fragrant flowers, gives good shade, and endures all difficulty and privation; common catalpa (*Catalpa bignonioides*), which is tough, fast

growing, has spectacular white flowers, fascinating long pods, and takes smog well; and Japanese pagoda tree or Chinese Scholar tree (*Sophora japonica* 'Regent'), which likes sun, needs well-drained soil, and gives good shade. These are the kinds of trees used to reclaim strip mines; they grow in situations otherwise classified as hopeless.

THE KINDERGARTEN PLANTS

In addition to the cast-iron plants are what I call kindergarten plants: flowers so easy to grow even the rankest beginner should have little difficulty with them. Mostly they are annuals, mostly they

American holly is a special joy in winter with its glossy, dark green leaves and red berries against the snow—a silent testament to the beauty of life, even in the darkest days.

Giant snowdrop is one of those satisfying plants that grows and blooms and spreads with no fussing or balking.

*Snapdragons are tall, attractive, easy, and reliable.
The perennial variety is susceptible to rust, and was
out of favor for a long time. It was replaced by the
annual hybrids, but recently, perennial snapdragons
have begun to make a comeback in American
gardens.*

are the plants found in your local nursery. They
are useful in the cottage garden to fill the holes left
by harvesting vegetables or gaps created by perennials past bloom. Classic kindergarten plants are
marigold, petunias, pansies, Johnny-jump-up,
snapdragons, cosmos, Zonal geraniums, Regal
pelargoniums, busy Lizzy, sweet alyssum (*Lobularia
maritima*), and morning-glory.

Other old-fashioned favorites, more commonly
found in garden catalogs and on seed racks than
at nurseries, are mignonette (*Reseda odorata*),
grown for its fragrance, yarrow, rose campion
(*Lychnis coronaria*), snow-in-summer (*Oerastium
tomentosum*), evergreen candytuft (*Iberis sempèr-
virens*), four-o'clock (*Mirabilis jalapa*), thrift
(*Armeria maritima*), and honesty, which is grown
for its silvery pods rather than its flowers. Nasturtiums, both the dwarf and the vining sorts, must
be planted from seed, since they refuse to be
transplanted. They're easy as pie: just poke the
seeds in the ground in the poorest soil in the sun-
niest spot you have. The dwarfs are good for bed-

ding and edging, the vining ones tumble recklessly
over walls, down precarious slopes, and hang off
cliffs in a manner that can only be described as
cavalier. Grown near the sea, where there is a lot
of moisture in the air, the leaves get the size of
saucers. Nasturtiums—the name is Latin for "nose-
twister"—are blessedly undemanding, and like
most of the flowers in this paragraph, they reseed
prolifically.

Sweet peas (*Lathyrus odoratus*) are invaluable in
a cottage garden. The bushy sorts need no stak-
ing or trellising: 'Jet Set' and 'Knee-Hi' are both
good varieties. The vining sort need string or wire
to wrap their tendrils around and climb on. If you
have an ugly chain link fence, plant it thickly with
the old-fashioned vining sweet peas. Soak the
seeds for several hours before planting to hasten
germination and plant them in the best soil possible (trench like the asparagus if the soil is uniformly
nasty). Given plenty of sun and plenty of water,
they will reward you for months with hundreds of
the sweetest-smelling flowers on earth. Pick huge
bouquets often; it's essential to keep the vines

*A profusion of sweet peas is a boon and a blessing
beyond price: They are such pretty pale pastels and
they smell so sweet!*

Morning-glory is a cottage garden classic. Nothing works better to create a country cottage effect than morning-glories on the fence, over the garden gate, or sprawling over the front door onto the roof.

Cottage gardens can be done in a single color scheme like this silver garden.

blooming. Picking sweet peas is one of those lovely instances where pleasure and prudence are one and the same, where what one wants to do is precisely what one ought to do.

ENTER THE HERB

Herbs are a traditional ingredient of the cottage garden. Many were used for medicines and healthful teas, what the French call *tisanes*. Others were used to add flavor to tough meats that had to be boiled for hours to render them edible or to distract from the fact that there were few means of keeping meat fresh. They gave variety to meals that were simple, and often the same day after day.

Like vegetables, many herbs are as ornamental as they are useful; in fact today more are grown for their simple attractiveness and sense of the past than for their practical applications.

Roses counted as herbs in the old cottage gardens, particularly cabbage or Provence roses, damask roses, and the apothecary rose (*Rosa gallica*). Peonies did as well, since peony seeds were used as a spice and believed to ease the pain of childbirth. Peony root was reputed to cure epilepsy and lunacy, too, not to mention its ability to ward off storms, devils, nightmares, and fear. No wonder it was known as "the blessed rose." Primrose leaves were used in salads, to ease the pain of childbirth, and to clear the complexion. Cowslip (*Primula veris*) is still used in northern Europe today as a sedative.

Sweet violets were then, and are now, pretty, fragrant, and useful. The leaves may be added to salads and the violets garnish salads or desserts such as custard, sorbets, and sherbets. The bright blue blossoms of borage are edible and may be floated in sweet punches or used to decorate tea cakes. The petals of pot marigold were used as a sort of "poor man's saffron," turning rice yellow as

saffron does, but without saffron's flavor. Saffron comes from the red stamen of the purple *Crocus sativus*: one ounce of saffron require the stamens of four thousand crocuses, which may give a clue as to why saffron was, and still is, expensive.

Sweet woodruff (*Galium odoratum*) dries with a scent like fresh-cut hay. Bunches of it tied up with a narrow satin ribbon are nice laid among the linens. Lavender tied in bunches and laid in drawers or on shelves leaves its lovely scent on sheets and towels and sweaters, and rosemary sachets do the same. Lily-of-the-valley is absolutely invaluable for its flowers and its fragrance. Not only does it naturalize where it's happy—my husband's mother has it growing by the acre—but its roots are still used to make a drug for heart disease similar to the digitalis from foxglove.

Peonies bloom best where winters are cold, and left undisturbed, will last several lifetimes.

Sweet basil is essential for pesto sauce and the perfect accompaniment to summer tomatoes, still warm from the sun.

Dill has delicate, fernlike leaves and flowers like yellow Queen Anne's lace. It is essential for making dill pickles and for chopping fresh onto grilled salmon.

If you grow pickling cucumbers, grow the dill to pickle them as well. Dill weed is quite tall, but there is a dwarf variety available that is better suited to small gardens. If you grow tomatoes, sweet basil is indispensable, for they are delicious together. Rosemary rubbed on a steak before grilling will have the neighbors over in no time angling for invitations to dinner.

Sage, rosemary, and thyme—all are easy to grow given what they like: poor soil, full sun, and drought. These, like the other herbs, can be tucked in the cottage garden wherever there's a bit of space. If the climate is too cold for them to get through the winter, sink them in pots, and bring them indoors for the winter.

Periwinkle was called "joy of the ground" in medieval times. It was believed to help one to "be happy and comfortable" and "to have grace," a state earnestly to be desired in the garden, and even without. The *Hortus Sanitatis or Gart der Gesundheit* (1485) *(The Garden of Health)*, declared, "Whoever carries this herb with him on the skin, the devil has no power over him, and no witchery may enter the house which has this herb hanging over the door . . ." Sounds simple enough; it's certainly worth a try.

Herbs come in all shapes and sizes. Fennel, dill, angelica, lovage (*Levisticum officinale*), yarrow, and pineapple sage (*Symphytum officinale*) are large, growing to four or five feet tall. Rosemary, sage, lavender, borage, and comfrey are from two to three feet tall. Cilantro and coriander (*Coriandrum*

A splendid profusion of the ornamental mixed with the edible: parsley, periwinkle, zinnia, and tarragon. Don't eat the periwinkle or the zinnia, and do enjoy the parsley and the tarragon.

Herb gardens can be very pretty and fragrant. Herbs must be kept neatly trimmed, or they sprawl and look untidy.

sativum), parsley, rue, marjoram, oregano, and mints rarely grow more than two feet high. Thymes, tansy (*Tanacetum vulgare*), and chamomile (*Chamaemelum nobile*) are low ground covers. Tucked in here and there, wherever they happen to fit, herbs belong in the cottage garden.

ACHIEVING SWEET DISORDER

When I planted my first cottage garden, I haunted the nurseries like a lost soul looking for old-fashioned flowers, laden with lore and rich with history that would grow in that "sweet disorder" the English have cultivated into a high art. I had every intention of planting randomly, tucking this here and that there, only to discover that years of vegetable gardening and life in a linear society have made deliberate disorder very nearly impossible for me. I have an orderly mind; the outward manifestation of this in the garden is neat rows. It took me hours of work to achieve the effect of happy chance, of casual beauty, of felicitous happenstance. Horticultural insouciance does not come easily to those of us who were taught that civilization is the process of imposing order on the universe.

It has been difficult to learn, appallingly late in life, that the universe has its own order, which suffers sadly under the yoke of human imposition. Cottage gardens come more easily to me now than they once did, but I offer my sobering experience as fair warning: The cottage garden has no place for the rigid, the inflexible, the controlling vision. It takes on a life of its own, and the gardener is admitted only as an observer who is privileged to watch the garden grow and flourish as it finds fit. Indeed, the gardener has little role past planting and harvesting, except to love.

CHAPTER SEVEN

THE MEADOW GARDEN

PERHAPS IT IS THE FACT OF HAVING GROWN up in the postwar suburbs of Southern California that shaped my passion for gardening. When I moved there, the land where I lived was still characterized by mile after mile of orange groves, olive groves, peach orchards, and walnut orchards. I remember driving past the orange groves when they were in bloom, the air so thick and heavy with the fragrance of orange blossoms that it seemed that all the world was sweet with it. Within twenty years all the groves had vanished, bulldozed to build housing tracts and shopping centers. A verdant, fertile land, rendered green and richly productive by irrigation, was transformed into grids of asphalt at right angles, every street lined with struggling lawns and not a mature tree for miles in any direction. I

127

longed for woods and meadows and tumbling streams with every fiber of my being though I had never known such things.

Time and water have worked their wonders on Southern California. It is far prettier today than it was when I grew up there, not because of the buildings, the vast majority of which are best described as architecturally undistinguished, but because the landscaping has matured and the trees have grown tall. Now the issues are far more urgent than simply those of urban and suburban ugliness. Today the burning question is whether there is enough water to sustain this sort of greenery in areas that are, by nature, deserts.

The question is not only applicable to Southern California, which is technically semiarid. It applies even more insistently to much of the land west of the one hundredth meridian, that magical meridian where rainfall drops to the point that agriculture cannot be sustained without supplemental irrigation. Much of that land is not merely semiarid, but truly arid. In the United States, vast tracts of the West, Far West, Southwest, and even parts of the eastern section of the Pacific Northwest are desert. Much of southern Europe is semiarid, much of north Africa, China, India, and Australia are arid. Nothing lives without water. Not plants, not animals, especially not people. For cities, suburbs, and for farms, there must be water, and it must come from somewhere else.

The story of the American West may someday be written in terms of riparian rights. Who owns water, who controls water, who needs water, who gets water. These are the questions that have dominated the human presence in the western United States since the first person stepped off the land bridge across the Bering Strait onto the North American continent.

Most of the people of the first nations solved the problem the way the animals did: they migrated. As nomads, they hunted and gathered whatever was native to the land. They did not settle, and because they were not bound to a single place, they did not plant. Wherever people settle, they plant food. Or perhaps it is that wherever people plant food, they settle. Anthropologists may argue the sequence one way or the other, rather like the question of the chicken and the egg, but the fact remains that people eat, ergo, they must have food, ergo, they must either find it growing naturally or grow it themselves.

To grow food, the land must be cleared of whatever grew there originally. In the United States, the forests that stretched from the East Coast to the Midwest were felled. The prairies of the Great Plains were plowed. And then agriculture bumped into the West. Insufficient rain made agriculture, even to support a single family, marginal or impossible, so instead cattle were run on the land. But as more settlers poured west looking for land and livelihoods, food had to come from somewhere, and the existing plants did not even begin to serve the need. The soil was not bad. The climate was good. All that was needed was water. So the settlers and their representatives in government set about shoving the rivers around to flow, not where they were, but where they were wanted: where the farms were.

Today California has not a single free-running river. There are not many in the West. Dammed and channeled and drained, water flows to farms. In California alone, 85 percent of the water goes to agriculture. Even with cities like Los Angeles sprawled all over dry lands, only 15 percent is used for people and gardens. Even if everyone replaced their lawn with xerophytic gardens, flushed only once a day, emptied their swimming pools, and took sponge baths, it still represents no more than 15 percent of water use in a state of twenty-six million people. The real issue is agricultural usage, and California would rather not talk about it, if you don't mind.

Similar issues arise wherever cities have sprung up on the basis of water from diverted rivers and diminishing aquifers. Can we sustain cities in the desert or will the desert dust one day blow through empty buildings abandoned to a dry and desolate land?

Given these parameters, what constitutes appropriate gardening, what is a sustainable ornamental landscape?

APPROPRIATE GARDENING

It is the right, indeed, the duty of gardeners everywhere to complain bitterly of the growing conditions against which they struggle daily. Where the climate is good, the soil is bad; where rocks litter the fields, the gardener longs for the deep loam of bottomland; where the soil is rich and easy to work, the gardener is wistful for a rock garden. Where the land is dry, we dream of bog gardens and pools of water lilies reflecting graceful willows, and where the land is natural marsh, we spend wildly to drain it dry. If the land is level, we call in bulldozers to make us pretty little hills and valleys; where it is sloped, we terrace at frightening expense to make it flat.

One method of appropriate gardening is to play it as it lays, to voluntarily limit one's efforts at reconstruction of the continental landmass, to work within the parameters of the existing land-

Wildflower meadow gardens usually include many native flowers that are sturdy, self-reliant characters that do well in most soils and bloom better without lots of water. This wildflower garden is in Santa Fe, New Mexico.

© Charles Mann

Ornamental grasses and daylilies like these are attractive and highly individual alternatives to the lawn-plus-foundation-plantings standard to suburbia. They also require substantially less money to plant, and far less time to maintain.

scape. At Hillside House, Herman Hein, one of northern California's leading landscape architects of the early part of the century, took a steep slope and terraced it elaborately to create level garden space. At Holly House, a similarly steep slope has been left entirely natural. The paths follow the original deer trails, widened somewhat. Plants are sunk in holes deep enough to hold water and small earthen berms are built to confine the water at the roots. Instead of conventional sprinklers, a drip-trickle system waters each plant individually. Those, like bulbs and native plants, that can manage on natural rainfall are left to their own devices. The idea is to work with the original contours of the land, to work within the context of the character of the land.

It is probably no longer possible to restore the vast forests of the East and West nor the wide prairies of the Great Plains; it is beyond our means to replicate or duplicate what once grew there in such abundance that the human mind could not encompass its richness. Still, within the scope of the garden it may be possible to suggest the beauty of the prairie, of tall grasses dancing in the wind, if not the stunning sense of space extending to the horizon and beyond. Where meadows and prairies were once the natural landscape, meadow gardens constitute appropriate gardening.

Native grasses have few significant pests since the virtual extinction of the buffalo and the antelope; in fact, even exotic ornamental grasses have few bug and caterpillar problems by comparison with other perennials. That means they don't need pesticides to look good. And meadow gardens require far less water than conventional lawns and gardens. Throughout most of the country most meadow plants can survive on natural rainfall. California, as always, is an exception: Meadow gardens in naturally dry areas need watering, though substantially less than is required to keep a lawn green.

Ornamental grasses function in a garden setting essentially as perennials do, with periods of new growth, flowering, and dormancy. Like some perennials, some grasses need good soil, good drainage, cutting back after dormancy, and watering in droughts; most do not. While meadow or prairie gardens need far less maintenance than the average lawn, one cannot buy a "meadow in a can," scatter the seed in spring, and legitimately expect to have a full-blown wildflower meadow by summer.

The preparation for a meadow garden is very similar to putting in a lawn: The soil must be tilled and raked smooth, it must be planted, watered, and weeded until the meadow grasses and flowers are solidly established. The maintenance is not similar at all: It is the difference between mowing once a week and mowing once a year, with no edging, dandelion digging, dethatching, fertilizing, or constant watering. To put this in economic terms, one prairie garden designer estimates that the cost of putting in a prairie garden is approximately half the cost of installing turf, and the maintenance costs approximately 90 percent less than the cost of maintaining a lawn. The difference in time and energy expended is about the same ratio: It takes about a tenth of the time as a lawn. A flowering meadow garden is so much lovelier than a struggling suburban lawn that there is no comparison, no logical method for calculating a percentage of beauty.

It takes a couple of years to get a meadow or prairie garden fully established. It must be weeded, as any garden must, of tree seedlings and rampant weeds. It must be raked after mowing to let the new growth emerge. Where there is plenty of rain, the meadow garden may need mowing more often, perhaps as much as three times a year, in late spring, late summer, and late fall. This is particularly true in the Northeast where the native landscape is deciduous forest. Left unmowed, a meadow in the Northeast will sprout with hardwood seedlings, and within five years, be a forest. (To which I say, let it, but if a meadow is what you are determined to have, it must be mowed.)

A grass garden is rarely all grass; it is more likely to be a garden where grasses are grown for their full-fledged beauty rather than sheared for a lawn. The early explorers told of prairies where the grass grew higher than a man's head, and tall grasses, native and exotic alike, are dramatic in an ornamental landscape.

A prairie garden is distinguished largely by the use of wildflowers and grasses native to the Great Plains of the Midwest: irises, wild roses, sunflowers (*Helianthus* spp.), coneflowers (*Echinacoea purpurea*), black-eyed Susans (*Rudbeckia hirta*), yarrow, asters, and goldenrod (*Solidago*). Other flowers that

grow without either summer water or winter protection are foxglove, cardinal flower, scarlet gilia or skyrocket (*Gilia aggregata*), Indian paintbrush (*Castilleja* spp.), blanket flower (*Gaillardia* spp.), gay-feather (*Liatris* spp.), camassia (*Camassia*), Joe-Pye weed (*Eupatorium purpureum*), beard-tongue (*Penstemon* spp.), Queen Anne's lace (*Daucus carota* var. *carota*), tickseed (*Coreopsis*), false indigo (*Amorpha fruticosa*), and wild onion (*Allium* spp.). Native prairie grasses are top-notch at surviving adverse conditions. Panic grass (*Panicum*), marsh grass (*Spartina*), beard grass (*Andropogon*), blue stem (*Schizachyrium*), grama (*Bouteloua*), prairie cord grass (*Spartina pectinata aureo-marginata*), and Indian grass (*Sorghastrum nutans*) come back year after year despite severe winters and hot summers.

East Coast meadow gardens are also heavily

The cardinal flower is native to North America in moist regions and damp boggy meadows.

The coneflower is native to the hot, dry Great Plains of the Midwest.

Black-eyed Susans, native to the United States, have it all—great name and looks, longevity in bouquets, and they're easy to grow.

mixed with native wildflowers: columbine, butterfly weed, bee balm (*Monarda didyma*), lupine (*Lupinus* spp.), strawflowers, sunflowers, gaillardia, yarrow, coreopsis, all sorts of asters, wild geranium, and spring beauty. Spring bulbs can be naturalized wherever their dying foliage will be covered by taller grasses. Good native grasses for the northeast and mid-Atlantic states are wild oats (*Chasmanthium latifolium*), woolly broomsedge (*Andropogon glomeratus*), and Indian grass.

In the Far West, including the Rocky Mountains, meadow gardens can be spectacular. Wild hollyhock (*Iliamna rivularis*), fireweed (*Epilobium angustifolium*), firecracker penstemon (*Penstemon eatonii*), meadowrue, cinquefoil (*Potentilla* spp.), larkspur, avalanche lily (*Erythronium grandiflorum*), western pasque flower (*Anemone occidentalis*), pearly everlasting (*Anaphalis margaritacea*), scarlet gilia, elephant-heads (*Pedicularis groenlandica*), horsemint (*Monarda menthifolia*), Western blue flag, tall bluebell, mountain bluebell and foothills bluebell (*Mertensia paniculata*, *M. ciliata*, *M. oblongifolia*), columbine, lupine (*Lupinus sericatris*), wild geranium (*Geranium* spp.), and yarrow are all good plants to grow in this region.

On the West Coast a meadow garden might include harlequin lupine (*Lupinus* spp.), sky lupine (*Lupinus nanus*), California poppies, cow parsnip (*Heracleum lanatum*), mule's ears (*Wyethia* spp.), shooting star, buttercup (*Ranunculus californicus*), owl's clover (*Orthocarpus purpurascens*), yellow Indian paintbrush (*Castilleja wightii*), Indian paintbrush (*C. franciscana*), Indian-warrior (*Pedicularis densiflora*), Mexican evening primrose and yellow evening primrose (*Oenothera* spp.), mullein (*Ver-*

Bluebonnets and paintbrush provide the wildflower color in this meadow. It begs for a picnic blanket, all the good food that can be crammed into a wicker basket, and two people to complete the scene.

Early spring bulbs like the bright yellow winter aconites grow easily in meadow gardens.

Purple crocus bloom in the early spring, before the grass has grown tall enough to hide their jewel-like beauty.

bascum spp.), grass iris, Ithuriel's spear (*Brodiaea laxa*), wild hyacinth (*B. pulchella*), blue-eyed grass, blue quamash (*Camassia quamash*), star lily (*Zigadenus fremontii*), farewell-to-spring (*Clarkia amoena*), larkspur, and penstamon. Grow yellow tarweed (*Madia elegans*) if for no other reason than how it smells after a rain. Good drought-tolerant grasses for California are beard grass, grama grass, panic grass (*Panicum virgatum*), flame grass (*Miscanthus sinensis*), prairie cord grass, and feather grass (*Stipa gigantea*). Native California grasses are California fescue (*Festuca californica*) and purple needlegrass (*Stipa pulchra*). Drought-tolerant grasses like big bluestem (*Andropogon gerardii*) and panic grass need watering to get through the first dry season; but once established they can sink roots twelve feet or more and manage with very little watering beyond natural rainfall.

A meadow garden is most interesting when it has a succession of bloom, wave upon wave of different flowers, each following in its season. The easiest way to achieve this effect is to combine native and cultivated plants. Meadow gardens look best mowed and raked in late fall or late winter, so the earliest bulbs can be used freely: The grasses will still be short enough when the bulbs bloom to see flowers. Winter aconites, snowdrops, glory-of-the-snow (*Chionodoxa* spp.), giant crocus, and "Tommies," as the British affectionately refer to *Crocus tomasinianus*, are all among the first to herald the advent of spring. Tommies and glory-of-the-snow both naturalize easily and quickly wherever they like the neighborhood.

Daffodils, narcissus, and early tulips are next in the procession of spring, and they, in turn, are succeeded by the late tulips, ornamental onions, and the first perennials: Shasta daisies (*Chrysanthemum superbum*), Oriental poppies, and the earliest of the grasses. Good choices for early-blooming grasses are *Calamagrostis arundinaoea stricta, fescue,* blue oat grass, and silky-spike melic (*Melica ciliata* and *M. transsilvanica*).

Summer meadows are alive with bloom from coneflowers, daylilies, giant alliums, lilies, *Rudbeckia fulgida* 'Goldsturm', threadleaf coreopsis (*Coreopsis verticillata* 'Moonbeam'), Turk's-cap (*Lilium superbum*), lilies, and yarrow. Fountain grasses like Chinese pennisetum (*Pennisetum alopecuroides*), panic grass, and bristle grass (*Setaria*), all come on in midsummer to join the *Calamagrostis arundinaoea stricta* and *Helictotrichon*, which are still blooming.

The coneflowers, both white and purple, continue their display well into the end of summer. Autumn asters, chrysanthemums, and Sedum 'Autumn Joy' combined with grasses such as flame grass, panic grass (*P. v.* var. 'Rotstrahlbusch'), and other large, dramatic *Miscanthus* species can round out summer handsomely.

Meadow gardens make a strong show in winter, in both color and silhouette. The fountain grasses (*Pennisetum* spp.) turn a pale almond color as does rush grass (*Sporobolus*). Panic grass and Indian grass both take on the golden color of wheat, and flame

Ornamental grasses add the quality of dramatic movement to a garden as no other plant can. They are remarkably easy to grow and maintain. This is **Miscanthus sinensis** *'Undine'* **(left)** *combined with* **Pennisetum alopecuroides (right).**

Black-eyed Susans (Rudbeckia fulgida *'Goldsturm'*) (left) *against the fence spell country charm. They bloom all summer and into fall.*

Daylilies (below) *are outstanding plants: easy to grow, adaptable to practically all soils and climates, and extremely long-lived. The clumps grow bigger every year and bloom heavily over a long period.*

grass turns from bright orange-red to soft orange. *Rudbeckia fulgida* 'Goldsturm' holds its bittersweet-chocolate brown seed heads well into winter, and *Sedum* 'Autumn Joy' does the same with seed heads the color of copper. Threadleaf coreopsis has an intriguing smoky gray presence, the eminence grise of the meadow in winter.

These lists, of course, are just for starters. There are many more wildflowers and cultivated flowers that grow well in meadows, and many more grasses as well. These merely give you some names to look for, some ideas to work with. Different flowers will flourish where the meadow is wet than where it is dry, so if you have significantly different levels of moisture in the soil, take advantage of it. Most meadow plants, whether wildflowers or cultivated, are pretty self-reliant characters. They can hold their own in competition with other plants and will thrive in almost any soil. Don't bother to amend the soil, and don't fertilize. Fertilizing just causes rank foliage and fewer flowers. Your local nursery will be able to help you choose the best plants for your garden.

FAIR WARNING

In the process of putting together the lists of flowers that might ornament a meadow garden in various regions, a nasty, niggling thought kept nagging at me. The thought is this: I don't know precisely how these various flowers behave in other regions. I do know that some plants that are well behaved in one setting can be absolute terrors in another. On paper, Scotch broom sounds like the ideal plant: pretty, bright yellow flowers, drought tolerant, adapts to any soil, takes sun or shade, reseeds readily. In northern California, where I live, it is a pernicious pest. The first time I saw it growing in a lovely garden near

Sissinghurst in England I was as startled as if our matronly British innkeeper had dressed herself in a G-string and danced across the lawn after breakfast. Scotch broom in northern California does not merely reseed itself; it is the only plant that I would willingly swear has a 150 percent recovery rate on viable seed. The California Native Plant Society excoriates it in nearly every issue of their newsletter, and exhorts its members to devote weekends to its destruction in wilderness areas where the Scotch broom is driving out native wildflowers.

Along with Scotch broom, California has eucalyptus trees. Native to Australia, the blue gum eucalyptus (*Eucalyptus globulus*) has naturalized as effectively as the Scotch broom. The difference, however, is significant; a weed that grows no more than ten feet tall (Scotch broom) versus a weed that can grow to four hundred feet and may live

Eucalyptus globulus *can live five hundred years and grow to four hundred feet, which is big for a weed.*

five hundred years (blue gum eucalyptus). I happen to know these interesting facts because when Holly House was built it had a sweeping view down the Ross Valley across San Francisco Bay to Mount Diablo. In the last twenty years some eucalypti planted down the hill have grown very tall. They have eaten the view of much of the valley and virtually all of the bay. I wistfully asked an old and dear friend, Dr. Ray Fosberg, now Botanist Emeritus at the Smithsonian Institution and one of the world's leading botanical taxonomists, when they would stop growing. That's where I got the four hundred feet or five hundred years, whichever comes first. I do not find this information reassuring. Above all, I do not want to be responsible for having suggested that someone plant something that could turn into a four hundred-foot weed. They are so difficult to pull at that size.

Every region has introduced plants and natives that are devilishly well adapted to a particular area; left to their own devices, nothing else would

Japanese honeysuckle grows fast, has pretty, sweet-smelling flowers, and attracts hummingbirds. Despite these good qualities, it has achieved noxious weed status in the East.

grow there. The East Coast has Japanese honeysuckle (*Lonicera japonica*), the South has kudzu vine (*Pueracia lobata*), Southern California has pampas grass (*Cortaderia jubata*), the Mother Lode country (Sierra Nevada foothills) has *Ailanthus* trees, all cases of perfectly good plants in perfectly the wrong place. Vita Sackville-West observed, "We often fail to remember that the treasures of our own gardens are the weeds of other lands." By the same token, the treasures of other lands may become weeds in our gardens.

If you have reason to suspect that Queen Anne's lace would soon form a solid stand in your meadow garden, don't plant it there. If you think that one of the flowers suggested would make your prairie garden look like the local weed lot, don't put it in. This is why no thistles made the lists, though many of them are very attractive. I even hesitated to include goldenrod, since its pollen so often stands accused of causing hay fever. The only reason the goldenrod made it in is the fact that a local allergist swore that goldenrod gets blamed for

© Charles Mann

Pampas grass has become a serious pest in Southern California, since it reseeds itself prolifically. It's huge, has razor-edged leaves, and is very difficult to eradicate.

misery more accurately attributed to ragweed (*Ambrosia*), which blooms at the same time. Local chapters of native plant societies or the Agricultural Extension Service can help set one straight on the difference between a pretty plant and a pest. It is worthwhile to avail oneself of their good offices.

THE DANCE OF THE GRASS

Grasses are the essence of the meadow garden. The flowers are seasonal, each blooming in its time, but the basic structure comes from grasses allowed to grow and bloom naturally. Full-grown grasses have a grace to them no other plant can claim as they dance with every breeze, and bow before the wind. They add a dimension of movement that is often absent from more conventional gardens. They catch the light of morning in a thousand different ways. Many grasses are colored: blue, green, gold, yellow, pink, red, even black. Some are striped. Some are delicately airy, like switch grass; some, like Moor grass (*Molinia caerulea arundinaoea* 'Windspiel'), are as dramatic in the landscape as a Calder mobile; some, like hare's-tail grass (*Lagurus ovatus*), have seed heads as soft and furry as a rabbit's tail. Job's-tears (*Coix lacryma-jobi*) has curious strings of shiny beads; the seed head of rattlesnake grass (*Briza maxima* and *B. minor*) looks surprisingly similar to a small golden rattlesnake's rattle. Flame grass, placed where it is backlit by the sun in fall when it turns brilliant orange-red, looks for all the world like a brilliant, blazing bonfire in the garden.

There is a tendency to associate prairie or meadow gardens (*prairie*, by the way, is the French word for "meadow") with wide open spaces, not exactly the sort of thing encompassed in the standard suburban lot. In fact, meadow gardens work wonderfully wherever lawns have been grown. The sense of spaciousness comes from the fact that the space is no longer broken up into lawn areas, flower beds, borders, foundation plants, and such. It's a lot like removing all the furniture from a room, refinishing and bleaching the hardwood floors, and taking down the drapes to let light flood in: all of a sudden, the room looks and feels substantially larger.

At the same time, large ornamental grasses can block the view at the ends and edges of the garden or provide privacy from encroaching neighbors. Bamboo, one of the most ornamental of all grasses, makes excellent hedges. Black bamboo (*Phyllostachys nigra*) is a dramatic screen anywhere temperatures don't drop below zero degrees F: it grows to twenty-six feet tall, which may be a tad taller than the average homeowner actually requires, but it can be trimmed to six to eight feet. (It is a running bamboo, the roots of which must be contained, or it will promptly proceed to take over the garden.) Massive grasses like giant miscanthus (*Miscanthus floridulus*), flame grass, maiden grass (*M. s.* 'Gracillimus'), and giant reed (*Arundo donax*) are all superb at arresting the eye and obscuring whatever needs to be obscured, whether hiding the back alley from view or creating a hidden nook within the garden.

Combined with equally imposing perennials, giant grasses can create the kind of privacy ordinarily associated with fences, stone walls, or dense hedges without violating the open feeling of the meadow. A good combination is *Boltonia asteroides* with giant reed or giant miscanthus, because the *Boltonia* covers up the bare legs of the tall grasses with masses of white flowers in late summer and fall. *B.a.* 'Pink Beauty' does the same in pink. Other excellent big perennials that combine well with the tall grasses are Matilija poppy (*Romneya coulteri*) with huge nine-inch crepe-paper-like white flowers; Jerusalem artichoke (*Helianthus tuberosus*),

Delphiniums (right) are not easy to grow: They need deep, rich soil, summer water, protection from wind, and stakes. However, all the work is richly rewarded when they bloom like these.

Plume poppies are splendid, with handsome foliage and blooms soaring eight or nine feet in the air. Excellent at the back of the perennial border, they are also a superb way to give a gazebo privacy.

which has edible tubers often retailed as "sunchokes"; cow parsnip (*Heracleum mantegazzianum*), which looks like a heavy-handed version of Queen Anne's lace; plume poppies (*Macleaya cordata*), which has superb leaves and plumes that fly like pennants seven or eight feet in the air—utterly unlike any other poppy on earth; foxtail lily that soars six to nine feet tall, punctuating the sky; Michaelmas daisy, a New England native that can grow to five feet, or Tatarian aster (*Aster tataricus*) that grows to six feet tall, both with flowers in the lavender-purple range.

Lilies are traditional in meadows. Indeed, all gardeners remember the lilies of the field with longing, for unlike gardeners, they do not toil or labor. The orange *Lilium henryi* grows to eight or nine feet; Humboldt lily (*L. humboldtii mag-*

nificum), also orange, grows to six feet tall; white Turk's-cap lily (*L. martagon album*) grows three to five feet tall; yellow Turk's-cap lily (*L. monadelphum*) grows to four feet tall; orange Turk's-cap (*L. superbum*) a native of eastern North America, grows to six feet and more; leopard lily (*L. pardalinum*), a California native, grows from four to eight feet tall, with flowers that open red or orange and fade to yellow; and Washington lily (*L. washingtonianum*), a West Coast native that grows four to six feet tall, with flowers that open white, fade to deep rose, and smell like a carnation.

More good tall flowers that work well with massive grasses are the familiar back-of-the-border flowers such as old-fashioned hollyhocks that tower nine feet tall; Giant Pacific delphiniums (*Delphinium elatum* 'Giant Pacific'), which can go to eight feet tall; and tree mallow (*Lavatera arborea*), fifteen feet tall, which is technically a shrub rather than a flower, but which might be very effective behind large grasses like *Miscanthus* at the farthest reaches of a meadow.

The wealth of material to choose from for a meadow garden is staggering. One nursery, Kurt Bluemel, Inc. in Baldwin, Maryland, grows more than five hundred grasses. That's before adding in the flowers native to your region, nonnative wildflowers, exotics from around the world, and cultivated ornamental flowers and hybrids, all of which are important elements of the meadow garden. It is worth visiting botanic gardens and nurseries that specialize in grasses to get a sense of how various grasses grow, and which would grow most felicitously in your area.

MEADOW WILDLIFE

Natural meadows are filled with birds, butterflies, and small, shy creatures. Because grasses provide excellent cover, material for nests, and seeds for

© Cary Pooler

All hummingbirds migrate to the United States from South and Central America, except the Anna's hummingbird on the West Coast. Hummingbirds are expanding their range north, so leave feeders up through the fall to catch a glimpse of those that come through too late to find flowers.

numbers of birds shift with the seasons. The more amenable the habitat, the longer the birds will pause on their journeys across the trackless skies. Like John (1699–1777) and William (1739–1823) Bartram three hundred years ago, in their garden near Gray's Ferry on the west bank of the Schuylkill River (now within the Philadelphia city limits), like Gilbert White in his garden in Selborne, England (A *Natural History of Selborne*, 1789), two hundred years ago, I watch eagerly to see the first visitant from faraway places: the rufous hummingbirds from South America, the bright warblers, the cedar waxwings, and Western tanagers from I know not where. The richness is in watching and wondering, and feeling oneself a part of the scheme of things.

food, birds often nest as well as feed in meadows. Monarch butterflies, which migrate thousands of miles, lay their eggs on butterfly weed and other milkweeds (*Asclepias* spp.). Mourning doves and dark-eyed juncos eat violet seeds; horned larks and Lawrence goldfinches eat the seeds of shepherd's purse (*Capsella bursa-pastoris*); and goldfinches, chickadees, house finches, titmice, juncos, and other songbirds all love sunflower seeds. Penstemons, foxglove, and columbine are food for hummingbirds, while owl's clover (*Orthocarpus*) and bee balm (*Monarda didyma*) attract flights of golden bees.

Meadows, because they offer food and shelter, often play host to birds of passage, the migratory birds that wing their way across wide continents and vast seas, for distances almost inconceivable to the human mind. Like the flowers, like the colors, like the changing light, the species and

ON THE EVOCATIVE NATURE OF THE MEADOW

It is important to remember that a meadow or prairie garden is not a natural meadow: It is an evocation of a meadow. Just as the Japanese use bridges over ribbons of rounded river rocks to suggest a stream where no water flows, a meadow garden is a meadow of the imagination with bloom and dramatic structure all four seasons of the year. It differs from conventional landscaping in the conspicuous absence of trees and shrubs, in flowers that are scattered rather than massed, and in grasses that are allowed to grow to full size and bloom. The purpose is to replicate a naturally occurring landscape in an enhanced form. It is a combination of textures, shapes, colors, and almost perpetual movement that pleases the eye, entices one's footsteps to wander in the meadow, and lures the mind to wander ever farther afield.

At the edge of a meadow, in a shady woodland glade, or in the border, foxgloves have the knack of belonging wherever they are. They also attract hummingbirds.

CHAPTER EIGHT

THE LITTLE GARDEN

I T HAPPENS, IN THIS ERA OF EXORBITANT housing costs, that people live in small spaces. Suburban houses are small, town houses are smaller, and apartments are smaller yet. The gardens are generally proportionate, until, in the apartment phase, they disappear entirely. Garden apartments may look out on a scrap of lawn and a few shrubs, but to have even that, apartment or condominium gardeners must consider themselves highly fortunate. Even if there is some small space—a miniature dooryard in front or private patio in back—one hesitates to landscape, simply because one is likely to move in a year or two. How does a gardener garden under these trying circumstances? The answer is to plant in containers.

In my first apartment I had no space but a tiny

landing on some back stairs. I bought a simple red-wood box four feet long and planted snapdragons and English ivy. The ivy trailed prettily over the box and the snapdragons made a spot of bright color. When I moved, the box went with me. Everywhere I went—and I have moved more than a dozen times—I found a place to put the planter and planted it with something bright and fresh. Recently it disintegrated, but not until it had served me long and well for nearly thirty years.

A BALCONY GARDEN

Given only a narrow balcony, say, five-by-ten feet, it is perfectly possible to have a pretty potted garden. Two big Chinese dragon pots, eighteen inches in diameter, twenty-four inches high, with

In a city apartment, sometimes the only way to garden is in containers.

a pair of fern pine trees (*Podocarpus gracilior*, often sold as *P. elongatus*) go in the two outer corners. In a narrow box six feet long, nine inches wide, and a foot deep, plant a passion vine (*Passiflora* 'In-cense') in the center and twine the tendrils in both directions along the posts and railing. 'Incense' is hardy to zero degrees F, evergreen through brief cold snaps (deciduous otherwise), has five-inch flowers that smell like sweet peas, and yellowish green oval fruit with a fragrant, tasty pulp. The fruit drops when it's ripe, so do keep them picked. In the remaining space of the box, put in annuals each season: yellow daffodils in spring, white impatiens in the summer, yellow chrysanthemums (*Chrysanthemum morifolium*) in the fall, and curly parsley through the winter. Plant the daffodils and parsley at the same time, when the mums come out. The parsley will look fresh and green all winter, and set off the daffodils nicely when they bloom in the spring.

If the view from the balcony is less than wonderful, block it with hanging baskets of flowers in the spring and summer: impatiens, ivy geranium, fuchsias, vining nasturtiums, Italian bellflower (*Campanula isophylla*), wandering Jew, or yellow archangel. They all grow splendidly in hanging baskets, and impatiens, nasturtiums, and fuchsias all attract hummingbirds as a bonus.

Passion fruit, of course, is edible as are the parsley and nasturtium leaves and flowers. Flower buds of the nasturtium can be used to make capers. Having created a little balcony bower with flowers, fragrance, fruit, and food, I would add a small table and a pair of chairs, where I would sit to have a cup of tea and read.

In spring I'd invite a friend or two over for a dinner of new potatoes with butter and fresh chopped parsley, mesclun salad with nasturtium leaves and petals, and grilled chicken brushed with olive oil topped off with homemade capers. Dessert, of course, would have to be a delicately

Planters, pots, and hanging baskets make a pretty garden of a small balcony or a rooftop.

scented passion fruit sorbet. I would tell everyone who would listen that it grew in my little balcony garden.

THE URBAN FARM

It is one of the conundrums of contemporary apartments, condominiums, and town houses that they often have kitchens with high-tech equipment that is *le dernier cri* (the last word), but no space to speak of to grow any of the things a good cook needs to have fresh and on hand to cook properly. Fortunately, it does not take an acre's worth of kitchen garden to grow herbs, a few fresh vegetables, and fruit. A sunny patio fifteen feet square will do just fine, along with some large containers, such as half-barrels. Half-barrels are big, sturdy, and inexpensive, all points in their favor.

Begin with the herbs. Plant a tall rosemary in the center two to three feet high, plant sage in a circle around the rosemary, garlic and chives in the next circle, and sweet marjoram, oregano, and several different sorts of thyme to tumble enthusiastically over the edges. All of these herbs, prefer sunny, dry conditions; the soil doesn't even have to be very good. A second herb barrel might have dill or coriander (also known as cilantro or Chinese parsley) in the center, sweet basil mixed with purple basils (the leaves of the purple varieties come ruffled or plain and the flavor is milder than sweet basil), and a variety of mints draping down the sides: spearmint (*Mentha spicata*), peppermint (*M. piperita*), orange mint (*M. aquatica citrata*), pineapple mint (*M. rotundifolia* 'Variegata'), apple mint (*M. suaveolens*), golden apple mint (*M. gentilis*), and pennyroyal (*M. pulegium*). This collection needs less sun and more water than the other. Rosemary, marjoram, oregano, thyme, sage, garlic, chives, and mint are perennials that need protec-

Window boxes and long planters grace this brick courtyard with bright flowers. They create a welcoming entry and a pleasant view for the house.

tion in cold climates. Basil and dill are annuals.

Next, the vegetables. Tomatoes are essential to summer, so give over two more barrels to tomatoes. One barrel could hold one bush of salad tomatoes and another bush of beefsteak tomatoes. The second might hold paste tomatoes for making spaghetti sauce and cherry tomatoes for antipasto plates.

I should announce here and now that growing tomatoes is a cult, with serious tomato gardeners indulging in activities bordering on the bizarre. If you have grown tomatoes successfully before, continue the practices, however peculiar, that led to your success. If you have not, a successful tomato grower will see that ignorance or failure written on your face the moment you mention your intention to grow tomatoes. He or she will take you under a wing, suggest strange rites, and whisper tomato secrets in your ear. Do whatever you're told, especially if this person's tomato credentials are good. (Impeccable tomato credentials consist of growing more than one's own family can eat, so if this person's friends and neighbors have been the recipients of bags and baskets and bushels of unsolicited tomatoes, do exactly as you're told. You, too, may one day know the unmitigated joy of carrying baskets of tomatoes into the coffee room at work, leaving a nonchalant note telling your co-workers to take as many as they like because there are more where those came from.)

Fortunately, growing tomatoes is not particularly difficult, as long as their terms are met. Tomatoes want good soil, monthly feeding, at least six hours of sun a day, plenty of water all summer long, and something to clamber over or on. Put a large wire tomato cage in the half-barrels as soon as the seedlings are a foot tall. Handpick tomato hornworms and stomp them or give them to your children to take to school in a jar for a science project in

Mint and sweet basil make a fragrant border for a small patio. In this small space lies the ingredients for fresh pesto sauce and iced tea with a sprig of mint.

Tomatoes that are commerically grown have absolutely nothing in common with the home-grown variety, which are so delicious in taste and texture that people eat them like apples.

metamorphosis. Choose varieties marked "VFN," which means they are resistant to verticillium and fusarium wilt as well as nematodes. Good paste tomatoes are 'San Marzano' and 'Roma'; good beefsteak tomatoes are 'Beefmaster (VFN)' and 'Big Girl (VF)'; good maincrop tomatoes are 'Better Boy (VFN)' and 'Ace'. Home gardeners can also grow golden tomatoes ('Jubilee' and 'Sunray'), white tomatoes ('Snowball' and 'White Beauty'), cherry tomatoes, plum tomatoes, or pear tomatoes (*Lycopersicon lycopersicum pyriforme*) in either red or yellow.

The theory in growing tomatoes is that it is possible to grow early, main crop, and late season tomatoes, thus measuring out the harvest evenly over spring, summer, and fall. In twenty years of consorting with expert gardeners, horticulturalists, farmers, and botanists, I have never met a single solitary soul who has managed to accomplish this. Typically one gets a few early tomatoes, a few late tomatoes, and an absolute inundation of tons and tons of ripe tomatoes in midsummer. When tomatoes are but seedlings, canned tomatoes, spaghetti sauce, tomato relish, tomato catsup, tomato chutney, even green tomato pie, all sound delicious, fun, and no trouble at all. In the breathless heat of midsummer, surrounded by piles of overripe tomatoes well past their first firmness, they sound like the worst idea anybody ever had. This is how fresh tomatoes end up in corporate coffee rooms. If you merely like tomatoes, plant no more than two vines; if you really love fresh tomatoes, plant four. More than four is agribusiness, and you'd better have eighteen-wheelers and a distributor lined up. One of the advantages of planting in a small space in containers is that one is protected from one's own enthusiasm by sheer lack of opportunity.

If you are really limited in space, grow the cherry tomato 'Sweet 100' in hanging baskets. It's more of a novelty than a crop, but it does take up a much less room than a half-barrel, it does produce lots of tomatoes, and I've seen it grown successfully indoors in front of a window.

Summer squashes are also prolific, particularly zucchini. In fact, zucchini is so prolific, it's hard to believe world hunger is a serious problem. Grow the bush types, not the sprawling vines. One zucchini or one yellow crookneck (*Cucurbita pepo Melopepo* 'Crookneck') will fill up a half-barrel, and look handsome all summer. You can solve some of the proliferation problem by picking the squash blossoms for stuffing: they're delicious, very Southwest, (which is to say, very fashionable at the moment), and in my opinion, better than zucchini. Pick zucchini religiously; a day or two of inattention, and they will grow to the size of a baseball bat. Sun, water, and regular harvesting are all they require. Winter squashes (C.

Scarlet runner beans have heart-shaped leaves, bright red flowers, edible roots, and can be eaten like either string beans or limas. They are a highly productive addition to the urban farm.

Lettuce and onions are a good combination: the onions help keep pests off the lettuce. For a longer harvest, pull off the outer lettuce leaves, and plant several varieties for mesclun, *the classic French salad of baby lettuce leaves and bitter greens, such as arugula.*

maxima) have about the same requirements, and they keep well into winter. One half-barrel could hold a 'Gold Nugget' a bush-type squash, or a 'Bush Table Queen', a bush-type acorn (*C. pepo pepo*) squash, both of which store well.

Another half-barrel can grow a fine batch of beans. Get six six-foot garden stakes, set them at an angle to form a tepee, and tie them together at the top. Plant two poles each of 'Kentucky Wonder', 'King of the Garden', and scarlet runner beans. The 'Kentucky Wonder' are green beans, snap beans, or string beans, depending on what you grew up calling them as a child, and 'King of the Garden' is a lima bean (*Phaseolus limensis*). Scarlet runner beans can be eaten as green beans or allowed to mature into beautiful purple and white beans to dry for winter. They also have edible tuberous roots to dig when the season's done.

In a corner that only gets morning or late afternoon sun, plant bush varieties of English peas (garden peas) (*Pisum sativum*), French *petit pois*, and snow peas (*Pisum sativum macrocarpon*) in early spring in cold climates, in fall, winter, and very early spring in mild climates. They prefer cool temperatures, consistent moisture, and good soil.

The peas will be over by midsummer, when you can put in potatoes. Order seed potatoes from a grower or cut sprouted potatoes into quarters. Bury them just under the soil and mulch them with a thick layer of straw. The plants will grow up through the straw, die back after a few months, and come fall, you can poke through the straw and find potatoes, harvesting without even getting your hands dirty. The earliest, little potatoes are prized as new potatoes, but the longer they're left, the bigger they'll get, right up to baking size. Just don't let them freeze or they turn to mush.

In two more half-barrels, plant one with a dwarf apple tree, the other with a dwarf pear. Beneath the trees go the greens: lettuces, spinach, and Swiss chard (one barrel with green chard, the other with red?). Or broadcast carrots; it will look as though the trees are growing in a bed of ferns. Or plant parsley, which also gives the effect of a bed of bright green beneath the tree. If you are willing to settle for pretty rather than edible, try Corsican mint (*Mentha requienii*). It's a mossy, dark green ground cover that smells glorious when it's touched and leaves its wonderful fragrance on your hands as well.

Carrots, beets, and radishes can be poked in wherever a bare place presents itself. Leeks, garlic, green onions, and chives are also good for tucking in here and there, and they help keep off bugs. Marigolds and calendula are good companion plants to slip in among the lettuce, spinach, and chard. They're bright, pretty, they discourage bugs

Parsley does well in deep planters; it has a long tap root. Unless you have the patience of Job, plant seedlings so you can pick it without waiting a discouragingly long time.

and the calendula petals add a nice note of color to summer salads. Both rhubarb and asparagus will also thrive in a half-barrel, as will peanuts (*Arachis hypogaea*) and Jerusalem artichokes (*Helianthus tuberosus*). This is, in fact, the ideal way to grow Jerusalem artichokes, since they're inclined to go rampant in the ground. In hot climates, plant jicama and sweet potatoes (*Ipomoea batatus*), and give the vines something to climb on, whether bean poles or green string up the side of the house. In ten half-barrels on a sunny deck, patio, terrace or even rooftop garden, one can have a small-space *potager*, complete with herbs, vegetables, and fruit, enough to eat all summer, and some to savor in the winter as well.

THE *ORANGERIE*

Growing citrus in formal pots is a tradition that has found its way pretty much all around the Western world from Spain to France to England to the United States. Citrus are particularly rewarding because they bud, bloom, and fruit simultaneously. The scent of citrus blossoms is one of the most extraordinarily heady flower fragrances in the world. They can be grown outdoors all year-round in mild-winter climates or as indoor/outdoor plants anywhere. Lemons (*Citrus limon*) and limes (*C. aurantiifolia*) require the least summer heat to produce good fruit, oranges (*C. sinensis*) and tangerines (*C. reticulata*) are in the middle, and grapefruit requires the most. In very hot climates, protect the trunk from sunburn with a water-based paint; commercial growers use white, but a brown close to the natural trunk color is less conspicuous in the garden.

Dwarf citrus are probably most practical for the small space garden, ranging in height from shrubs four feet tall to small trees ten feet tall; standard citrus grow twenty to thirty feet tall and as wide,

Citrus trees are excellent container plants, whether oranges, lemons, tangerines, calamondin or grapefruit. A collection in matched pots is called an orangerie.

Dwarf Valencia oranges grow well on sunny patios, balconies, rooftops, or in courtyards—anywhere the pot or planter will fit. The flowers are wonderfully fragrant, the leaves are glossy, and the fruit is delicious.

which makes bringing them in for the winter a bit daunting. Stick to the dwarfs: there are more than thirty varieties of citrus available in dwarf rootstocks. Oranges are wonderful to bring in for the winter because they bloom in November, making whole rooms smell sweet, and they ripen in December and February. They'll do fine in a conservatory, sunroom, sun porch, or any bright room where the temperature stays above freezing.

To create a formal *orangerie*, use matching pots. The white wooden Versailles boxes are traditional. In a Spanish-style courtyard, use large terracotta pots. In a very contemporary setting, citrus trees in black glazed ceramic cylinders have a striking effect. Traditionally, the trees are pruned to the same size and shape, and placed in neat rows. They are dramatically effective at lining an entry, filling a courtyard, or introducing a note of formality on a tiled terrace. Benches at the ends or along the sides of the *orangerie* provide a pleasant place to bask in the sun or delight in the fragrance.

There is a lovely *orangerie* at the Royal Botanic Gardens at Kew just outside London, and another in the front courtyard of *La Biblioteca Nacional* in Seville, Spain, across the street from the cathedral. At Kew, one may have tea in *L'Orangerie*, and in Seville, one may rest from one's wanderings with a stroll among the sweet-smelling trees.

THE TOWN HOUSE PATIO

It was nothing but a slab of concrete with three plywood walls. Someone had once attempted to earn salvation by building some crude wooden planters at the base of the walls, but whatever had been planted there had long since gone to join its Maker. A sliding glass door from the dining room opened onto it and the kitchen window looked out to it. A gate led out to the carport behind the building. That was the twelve-foot by fifteen-foot "backyard" of the town house. To call it depressing would have been an effusive compliment.

Clearly something had to be done to make this nasty little bit of undiluted urban ugliness into pleasant, useful space. But what? Replacing the walls was out of the question—they were common walls with the neighbors on either side. Tearing up the concrete slab was equally out of the question—it was forbidden under the covenants of the Homeowner's Association. A well-lobbed hand grenade didn't seem like quite the right solution either, though the idea was proposed and given thoughtful consideration on more than one occasion.

The first chore was to tear out the existing planters, piling all the soil in the middle of the concrete patio. That exposed an eight-inch strip below the walls filled with dirt and construction rubble in which the fence posts were set. The amount of work required to dig it out and replace it with good soil was intimidating. There was also some genuine concern about undermining the fence. Once done, there still wasn't room enough to plant much of anything.

This town house garden has all the right elements: plenty of potted flowers, a little waterfall to mask neighborhood noise, and a still pool to reflect the sky and trees.

Lots of annuals brighten this summer container garden: zinnias dahlias, gomphrena, sedum, and cosmos. This garden could fit in a tiny dooryard or a small balcony.

Moving swiftly to Plan B, a carpenter was hired to build new, freestanding redwood planters eighteen inches wide and two feet deep on three sides of the patio. Each planter was three feet long, an easy size to take along if the owners moved. Good compost and slow-release fertilizer were added to fresh soil, and the new planters were planted with dark green English ivy, the tendrils tacked against the plywood walls.

A large Boston ivy in an eighteen-inch basket weave concrete pot was placed against the stucco wall of the town house between the sliding glass door and the plywood fence, the vines carefully tacked to the stucco until they came to cling by themselves.

At the opposite diagonal corner, a ten-foot Mayten tree (*Maytenus boaria* 'Green Showers'), a

Handsome terracotta pots (top) filled with perennials need to be planted only once. Annuals need to be replaced as soon as they're past bloom.

The easiest container plants of all are cacti (above) all of which are succulents, but not all succulents are cacti. However, both require little water and are far better at tolerating high temperatures than most annuals and perennials.

broadleaf evergreen, in a twenty-four inch basket weave concrete pot was installed. This was only after much agonizing over which tree to plant, for the tree had to be in scale with the small space, and it needed to provide some shade since summer temperatures often went to one hundred degrees F and higher. A broadleaf evergreen was best to absorb noise and dust year-round from a nearby freeway, but it would have been wonderful to have had spring bloom, summer fruit, fall color, and an interesting bark pattern as well. Alas, no one tree does everything. The size, the shape, the shade, and the fact of being a broadleaf evergreen were the most important criteria, so the mayten it was. Mayten trees look something like a weeping willow, creating very much the same sense of cool green shade, but are smaller and much better behaved: no growing into water pipes, no heaving up concrete, no dropping leaves all over the place.

A hand-blown clear glass hummingbird feeder that glows ruby red when the sunlight strikes the nectar was the tree's "welcome home" present, hummingbirds being of the proper proportions for this garden. Nothing but hummingbirds, winter wrens, bushtits, chickadees, and kinglets are really built to scale for this space; a jay in the tree would look like a hawk.

The English ivy in the planters now covers the plywood walls in dark green leafiness, a few stems trailing gracefully over the sides of the boxes. Wherever there is a bit of space between the ivy, white Cascade petunias tumble over the edge of the planter boxes, blooming flamboyantly. A small arch built over the gate supports a 'New Dawn' climbing rose that grows over the arch and along the top of the back wall, flinging sprays of pale pink roses about with wanton abandon. The rose, like the Boston ivy, is potted into a large basket weave concrete pot. Three smaller basket weave pots massed together in a corner serve as cache-pots for chrysanthemums for Thanksgiving, poinsettia (*Euphorbia pulcherrima*) at Christmas, cyclamen for the New Year, paperwhites on Groundhog Day, lilies at Easter, and more petunias from May Day through Labor Day when it's back to mums again.

Redwood duckboard placed over the concrete slab creates the effect of a redwood deck, not permanent, but like the pots and planters, portable. Besides looking infinitely more attractive, the duckboard reduces the amount of reflected summer heat substantially, making both the patio and the house cooler and more pleasant.

Surrounded by the Boston ivy, a recirculating terracotta dolphin wall fountain hangs on the stucco wall. The sound of gently falling water helps drown out the noise of neighbors and traffic. In fall, the Boston ivy turns flaming scarlet, and in winter, makes a subtle tracery on the wall.

While the work on the patio was being done, a hanging basket of especially lush ivy geranium improved the view from the kitchen window by eliminating it entirely. When the little garden was finished, and the view very much more attractive, a window box was added under the kitchen window. The ivy geranium was planted in it, where its pink flowers match the pink of the 'New Dawn' rose.

It looks quite lovely, but it had a dark history, for the cook of the house had set his heart on having an herb garden in the window box, and had indulged in many a delicious daydream about snipping fresh herbs through his kitchen window. The mistress of the house preferred to look at flowers blooming over her sink. Tragedy was averted, and all parties gratified when a terracotta strawberry jar with rosemary, marjoram, oregano, silver-leaf thyme, lemon thyme (*Thymus seapyllion*), sage, tarragon, and chives was installed next to the door, only steps from the kitchen.

This garden refuge is furnished with a small dark green table and chairs of the sort used at sidewalk cafés in Paris. The table is barely big enough to hold a pair of cappuccinos or cafe lattes and a good book or two. From both the kichen and the dining room, the garden makes a charming view. As an entry to the house from the carport, it is like stepping into another world from the moment the gate swings open. Other than a kiss and a hug from someone you love, it's the nicest sort of welcome home.

GARDEN OF SERENITY

The Japanese figured out how to create the illusion of serenity a long time ago: put the emphasis on shape, stick with a single color palette, and use only natural materials. The shapes are rounded or gracefully curved—Nature and Japanese gardeners abhor straight lines just about equally. The color palette is shades of green—every nuance of tone and texture is examined and exploited. The natural materials are water, wood, bamboo, and rocks, and plants—consider how they will look wet and dry, how a rough rock looks paired with glossy leaves, how a bamboo fence sets off the planes of the Japanese maple, how each element balances the other. The purpose is always to suggest a vast landscape in a small space. It is also to suggest separation and isolation from the world outside. It must have the look of age, as though it had always been as it is and would always be thus. It is simplicity pared to the bone. Simplicity and serenity have a lot in common, both philosophically and horticulturally.

Simplicity is not simple. I cannot tell you how to build a true Japanese garden. I don't know. While the garden may be the essence of simplicity, the symbolism is endlessly complex. The Japanese have a garden tradition that stretches back over a thousand years, and I know only a small part of that history and tradition. What I can do is suggest how to create a garden that looks like what an American thinks a Japanese garden looks like, a garden that reflects what Western eyes see when they look at a Japanese garden.

The first thing the Western eye observes is how different Japanese gardens are from American or English or Continental gardens. There are no flower borders, no children's sandboxes, no berms with the house number spelled out in succulents. The Japanese garden is as much about what isn't there as what is. It is not "useful" in the sense that Westerners employ that term. Space is not allotted for patio tables, cold frames, or storing the ski boat. It seems reasonable to assume that Japanese people must have such things somewhere, but they do not put them in their gardens. Japanese gardens, on the highest plane, are about achieving spiritual enlightenment, not having the neighbors over for a barbecue. At the very least, a Japanese garden is a place of quiet observation. One does not stroll in the Japanese garden with one's cellular phone shouting instructions to one's broker in order to make a fast killing; one prepares one's mind to be quiet and receptive, to contemplate and meditate on nature and the eternal verities.

The first job is to walk the perimeter of the backyard to see what scenery is there. Is there a view of hills or a neighbor's tree? How can they be framed to give the small garden the sense of a sweep of greater space? Is there a way to draw the eye beyond the garden proper? How can the garage next door or the dog run be camouflaged? The idea is to suggest a broad natural landscape within the parameters of a small yard, exactly as bonsai suggests mountains and ancient trees within the miniscule dimensions of a bonsai pot. Think of the Japanese garden as an oversized bonsai pot.

The garden I am going to describe never made it into existence. It is, however, a good description of how a small ordinary yard can be transformed into a Japanese garden. The garden was designed for a two-story Victorian. Unfortunately, the house was sold before the garden was finished.

The backyard was thirty feet-by-forty feet, not much more than a dog-ravaged lawn with a dying cherry tree and one huge pine. It sloped uphill slightly, and at the high end, had a stone wall three feet tall. The terrace above the wall was six feet wide, with a few bedraggled bearded irises. Like the lawn, the dog had romped over the irises, and since irises generally do not take foot-traffic well, they looked rather the worse for wear. A weathered six-foot redwood fence surrounded the yard on three sides. The yard was entered from a wooden gate at the low side of the yard, and from steps that came down from the upstairs apartment.

The neighbors on the uphill side had a viburnum (*Viburnum*) that colored spectacularly in the fall in every possible shade of red. In the distance, a ridge of wooded hills stretched the view out to the sky. Both the hills and the viburnum were incorporated into the design.

All the dead wood was pruned out of the old

Shugakuin Imperial Garden in Japan is an outstanding example of the sense of serenity evoked by classic Japanese gardens.

Japanese snowball has clusters of white flowers in the spring, leaves that turn purplish red in the fall, and an attractive horizontal branching pattern in the winter.

cherry, leaving most of the branches all on one side. It was carefully trimmed to create a cascade effect with long branches sweeping nearly to the ground. The pine was thinned for a more dramatic silhouette, forming alternating planes of dark branches and light. The patterns of light were plotted on the ground to see where the shafts of sunlight through the tree fell on the ground as the sun passed through the sky. All the irises were dug, dozens of rhizomes, which had not been divided for thirty years or more; the neighbors were delighted to have them as a gift.

The owner wanted a teahouse garden (*Cha-niwa*) "with some water somewhere." The teahouse was designed as simply as possible to be nine feet-by-twelve feet (the size of six three foot-by-six-foot *tatami* mats, more familiar to Americans as beach mats, but originally the basic unit of measure for all traditional Japanese houses), with translucent rice paper sliding *shoji* screens on all sides and a blue glazed tile roof. It was placed in the far corner of the yard, a few feet from the stone wall, parallel with the back fence.

To block out the neighbor's garage on the low side, a hedge of golden bamboo (*Phyllostachys aurea*) was suggested. It makes a dense, golden green screen, takes drought well, and is hardy to zero degrees F. It grows naturally to twenty feet, but can be kept to six feet to ten feet without difficulty. The golden green contrasts well with the very dark green of the pine and provides good textural contrast with the bark, shape, and color of the cherry. It needs a piece of metal flashing sunk to a depth of three feet at the outer border to keep it from running wild and sprouting all over the yard. The same technique was used to screen the duplex from the garden: golden bamboo growing through gravel.

Japanese often put gravel at the base of bamboo groves, and each spring, select only the best placed shoots to grow, rooting out all the others. Americans generally let the shoots grow as thickly as they like, only removing dead canes.

Since the pine cast afternoon shade along the back fence, black bamboo (*P. nigra*) was chosen to grow there. The lowest branches of the pine dipped just below the top of the fence. To keep the pine silhouette clean, the black bamboo began at the outer edge of branches, just beyond the drip line. Black bamboo is smaller and more delicate in feeling than the golden bamboo, and while it can grow to fifteen feet, it was intended to be kept between eight and ten feet. It extended from the outer edge of the pine behind the teahouse to the stone wall, and it, too, needed to be confined with a three foot metal flashing. It is hardy to five degrees F. Beneath the black bamboo were several varieties of moss, to enhance the sensation of cool, quiet shade. The shafts of sunlight that penetrate the pine highlight the shining black canes of the black bamboo grove. It also casts graceful, leafy, shifting shadows on the *shoji* screens at the back of the teahouse.

Along the top of the stone wall terrace heavenly bamboo (*Nandina domestica* 'Umpqua Chief') was planted. Not a true bamboo but a member of the barberry (*Berberis* spp.) family, its leaves look like bamboo, but it does all sorts of wonderful things bamboo does not. It has airy sprays of white flowers, turns fiery crimson in fall, holds its leaves all winter unless the temperatures drop below five degrees F, and has bright red berries through the winter. It is hardy to ten degrees F, though if it dies back to the ground it comes back quickly in the spring. It grows well in restricted areas and reaches a height of six to eight feet.

With the black bamboo kept at eight feet and the heavenly bamboo kept at six feet, both the neighbor's viburnum and the ridgeline of the wooded hills remained visible, yet all sign of the neighbors was eliminated. The Japanese snowball (*Viburnum plicatum plicatum*) has two-to-three inch white flowers in the spring, a handsome horizontal branching pattern in the summer, and purplish red leaves in the fall. The horizontal lines echo the line of the hills and contrast with the vertical lines of the heavenly bamboo over which it is seen. At fifteen feet tall and as wide, it draws the eye beyond the boundaries of the yard, up and over the boundaries of the heavenly bamboo it grows behind.

In front of the heavenly bamboo, white azaleas were massed to fill the terrace, trimmed in the Japanese style of rounded mounds. Again the rounded lines contrasted well with the vertical lines of the heavenly bamboo, as did the dense,

Heavenly bamboo has airy sprays of tiny white flowers followed by scarlet berries that last through winter.

dark green masses against the airy nandina.

About two-thirds of the way down the terrace from the back fence, a recirculating pump pushes up water in a natural-looking spring. The water tumbles over the edge of the wall onto carefully chosen rocks, flows in a small three-to-five-foot wide stream across the yard, and ends in a pool bordered by the golden bamboo at the opposite side. Spring, stream, and pool are planted with small ferns, white and purple Japanese iris (*Iris kaempferi*), blue plantain lily (*Hosta ventricosa*), and mosses. The pool has a few water lilies, some reeds, and five large *koi* (Japanese carp). (The pool has

Hostas give a rich, luxurious look to shady nooks and moist places. Grown for their foliage, the leaf color can range from new-willow green to yellow-green to blue-green and many are variegated with white or yellow markings.

ledges for the *koi* to hide under when the inevitable raccoon raids are staged.)

Near the center of the yard, between the teahouse and the edge of the pine, is the maple forest. Nine Japanese maples grow in a grove through which the stream meanders. The grove permits only glimpses of the teahouse between the trunks of the trees. A stepping-stone path (*tobi-ishi*) from the gate leads past the cherry tree, whose branches are reflected in the stream and almost touch the water, across the stream in the maple forest, curving at last to a stone lantern (lighted only with candles) and stone water basin in front of the teahouse. In the narrow space between the teahouse and the stone wall are a fern pine and several Japanese aralia (*Fatsia japonica*). The gate at the opposite end of the path is framed by a pair of white single-flowered Sasanqua camellia (*Camellia sasanqua*).

Because the old cherry is dying, three younger cherries grow in a triangular clump between the old cherry and the pine. They are small, but they will have a substantial presence by the time the old cherry dies completely. One of the trees is positioned so its branches will one day be reflected in the stream.

Except for the stepping-stone path, the paths in this garden are swept dirt bordered by curved bamboo. One leads from the back stairs past the young cherries to the pine. The same path curves past the golden bamboo beside the house to the waterfall. A small weathered redwood garden seat is placed near the waterfall, and another under the big pine. To give the redwood fence the look of a traditional Japanese *itabei* (plank fence), a small roof cap was placed at the top for its entire length. The ground covers are many kinds of mosses.

This is a spare garden. Its predominant color is green, though many shades of green, from golden green to blue green to gray-green to very dark green. There is movement from the water and the bamboos, there is textural contrast between the soft mosses, the shiny leaves of camellias and Japanese aralia, and the matte finish of the leaves of the fern pine. There is the sound of the wind in the pine and the tumbling water of the waterfall. The camellias bloom in winter, the cherry blossoms and azaleas in spring, the irises in summer. The maples and heavenly bamboo color in the fall, the heavenly bamboo carrying its color through the winter.

It is a simple garden, a serene and peaceful place for quiet contemplation. It has, I hope, the qualities of *sabi* and *wabi*, so cherished by Japanese tea masters: *sabi* is the appearance of age, antiquity, rusticity, and natural textures; *wabi* is the sense of solitude, tranquillity, and quietness. This little garden was designed to bring about that state wherein by losing oneself in thought, in observation, in meditation, one finds oneself.

This enchanting meditation house looks out on a gently moving stream bordered by Japanese iris.

CHAPTER NINE

THE IMPASSIONED GARDENER

H INTS AND INSINUATIONS HAVE BEEN WOVEN through this book, but I have decided to face the issue squarely and confess: I am a lazy gardener. Over the years I have devised any number of ways to neatly sidestep garden chores I hate. Spraying, whether pesticides, fungicides, or herbicides, is one to which I've already admitted. Instead, I pick off caterpillars and squash them, throw cutworms, slugs, and snails as far as I can fling them over the fence, and wash off aphids with a hard spray from the hose. The best disease and pest control is good healthy plants and regular maintenance.

I pick off the leaves of roses that have black spot or rust and put them straight into a covered trash can. I prune out diseased and deadwood on trees and shrubs, and stick it in the trash as well. There is an important distinction to be made between pruning and outright mutilation. I do not subscribe to the Lizzie Borden school of pruning, which means I do the absolute minimum that I can get away with. (For those not familiar with the annals of American crime, Lizzie Borden was immortalized in the little ditty "Lizzie Borden took an ax/Gave her mother forty whacks/When the job was nicely done,/She gave her father forty-one." In the interests of justice and fairness it must be added that Lizzie was aquitted.)

The composting is done as minimally as the pruning. Leaves and grass are dumped in a pile, watered now and then during the dry season, and that's about it. On those rare occasions when the fact of a visitor shames me into raking the paths, the leaves go straight to the compost heap. Occasionally, in a fit of inexplicable righteousness, the wood ashes from the fireplace are added to the pile and watered in. This may be the world's most casual compost heap, but it makes perfectly good compost. Here in California it is illegal to burn leaves, but more than that, it's a waste of a useful resource. I believe in returning to the earth anything it's willing to take back. Since nature does all the work, composting takes no time or trouble. Composting enriches the soil, burning pollutes the air. That makes the decision fairly uncomplicated.

Mulching improves the soil, reduces watering by reducing evaporation, keeps down some weeds, and is a way of recycling wood chips, spoiled hay, or leaves. Ground covers can accomplish a lot of the same purposes and absorb dropped leaves as well, which cuts down significantly on the raking. Rotted manure may be had by the bucketful, bagful, or truckful from most riding stables. It's usually free, and it can be tossed on the compost heap, dug into the garden, or simply scattered as topdressing.

Planting trees creates shade, which reduces the amount of watering necessary. It also opens up

Providing the birds with water means there are more birds in the garden, fewer insects, and more birdsong in the morning.

more options on what will grow in the garden since more plants do well in partial shade or filtered sun than full sun. Planting perennials is a one-time thing: you do it once, not every season. My duties are restricted to watching them grow, a job for which I seem to have a natural flair.

The water is on a drip-trickle system with an automatic timer. It waters at night during the dry season and not at all during the rainy season. The sprinkler heads need to be checked regularly to make sure they're working properly and the lines inspected for raccoon damage. Strolling through the garden quickly makes it clear if there are any leaks or plugged-up sprinklers.

The weeding is done each time I wander through the garden. I pull up the Scotch broom seedlings or mark the poison oak sprouts for death and destruction. I use metal plant markers to identify the places where the dormant have done their disappearance. It keeps me from digging them up accidentally and from tromping on tiny new shoots. All earthworms and night crawlers inadvertently unearthed are blessed and returned to the soil to go about their business of aerating and enriching it.

The birds are encouraged with seed feeders, winter suet, hummingbird nectar, and birdbaths. In return, they keep insect pests to a tolerable level. The garden is fenced against the devastations of the deer, and when they manage to get in anyway, shouting and arm waving and false charges usually send them gracefully leaping over the fence and into the woods. If gardening gets any easier—or lazier—than this, it is only because I have not yet figured out how.

A CONTEMPLATION ON CATALOGS

There is one more way in which I make my gardening easy. I order a few catalogs of seeds, bulbs, plants, and garden tools, and those only from companies that have proved themselves absolutely reliable. It cuts down substantially on the disappointment of seeds that don't germinate, plants that don't grow, and tools that don't work.

The best seed catalogs in the United States are those of the W. Attlee Burpee Company, George

W. Park Seed Company, and Thompson & Morgan. The best plant catalog is White Flower Farm in Litchfield, Connecticut; the plants can be counted on to arrive in good condition. The catalog is a treasure house of information on the culture of ornamentals, particularly for the eastern half of the country. An excellent and extensive catalog of bulbs is found in the K. Van Bourgondien & Sons catalog. Smith & Hawken also has a bulb catalog that is very, very good *and* environmentally responsible in terms of verifying the sources of their bulbs. (So many bulbs have been collected in the wild, that some species are threatened in their native lands. Bulbs are better commercially grown than collected, especially rare and unusual species.) The best modern roses are from Jackson & Perkins, the best "antique" roses to be had are from Roses of Yesterday and Today. Burpee's, Park's, and Thompson & Morgan all offer excellent selections of vegetable seeds as well. The best herb and rare seeds catalog is Nichols. The best bog and water garden plants catalog is from Lilypons Water Gardens. The best gardening equipment catalog in America, bar none, is Smith & Hawken. (The addresses for all of these catalogs and many more sources begin on page 177.)

In addition to tools, there are miscellaneous garden items that have proven invaluable in my garden. Inconspicuous metal stakes covered with dark green plastic in different heights and metal plant markers, both from Smith & Hawken, are two that come readily to mind. Every garden has different requirements, every gardener has different interests. What is useful in my garden may be pointless in yours. In the long run, it is less expensive, less time-consuming, and just generally easier to use products that do the job they were bought to do. Even if you are no more than an armchair gardener, these catalogs are a winter night's delight to read.

A BRIEF DISSERTATION ON DESIGN

My father grew up thinking gardening was being told to rake the lawn, weed the flower beds, and water the lawn, no more, essentially, than a long list of hateful chores that kept him from tramping about in the woods he loved. It was his firm conviction, at least during my childhood, that one of the primary purposes for producing children was so *they* could rake the leaves, weed the flower beds, and water the lawn. I did not share his conviction, however firmly held. Yet nurseries with all their flats of flowers fascinated me.

I remember, with the vividness that only excruciating embarrassment can give a memory, my first garden. I was six years old, and my parents had a standard suburban lot landscaped in typical suburban style: foundation plantings around the house, a lawn, and a sycamore tree plunked precisely in the middle of the lawn. Even at that tender age, I knew that was not the sort of garden I had in mind.

Instead, I imitated the only other plantings I had ever seen, the dreadful annuals beds of public parks. I planted, very earnestly, a section of side yard, four feet wide and ten feet long, to look like the American flag. I chose my pots of seedlings with utmost care: blue floss flower (*Ageratum*) (though I was troubled that the blue was wrong, being far too pale), white sweet alyssum, and red, heavily fluted cockscomb (*Celosia cristata*), so the flag would look as though it were waving in the breeze. I vaguely recall that I was awarded a prize

This is a beautiful example of the Spanish tradition of gardening, the walled courtyard giving privacy, the graceful arcade providing cool shade, and the tiles and wrought-iron gate setting off the flowers.

for this stunning horticultural achievement, though what august body awarded the prize or on what grounds, I have no recollection. Perhaps the prize was for patriotism. It was not, I feel quite certain, for gardening.

I did learn some important things from that garden. I learned that it can be difficult to find exactly the blue one needs for a particular spot in the garden. Even with all the blue flowers I know today—delphinium, canterbury-bell, bachelor's-button, blue poppy, balloon flower, bearded iris—none of them are quite the blue of the American flag. They are certainly not the right size or shape. I learned that coordinating the size and shape of different plants is a challenge all by itself. I discovered that some use may be made of a side yard besides trying to pretend it isn't there. While I have no plans for repeating the experiment, it was highly informative.

The challenges that I faced then of coordinating color, size, and shape to create a particular effect are essentially the same challenges every gardener faces. To do it well means growing a lot of plants and making mental notes about which do well and which will never darken your doooryard again.

It means knowing what a plant looks like at maturity as well as when you plant it. It was popular when I was growing up to plant Italian cypress at the front corners of the house. The houses were single-story California ranch-style in the endless rows typical of tracts. The cypresses have continued to grow over the years and now tower ten or twenty feet over the houses. Italian cypresses have dignity and strength planted in double rows along the drives approaching Italian villas, but they look sadly disproportionate when they're twice as tall as a tract house. Camellias planted as foundation plants now, thirty years later, press against the eaves, block all the windows, and make the house dark as a tomb.

Trees and shrubs that are cute when they are

little, or the perfect size at adolescence, may be substantially less appealing when they are mature. It's worth finding out how big things get and how long they take to get that way sometime prior to the day they have to be transplanted because they've outgrown their place in the garden.

THE GOOD PLANTSMAN

The greatest compliment that one landscape architect, garden designer, or gardener can give another is to call them "a good plantsman." Gertrude Jekyll was one of the best, the inappropriateness of language to gender notwithstanding. She knew how plants grow: how tall, how bulky, how adaptable, how fussy, how sturdy, how brittle. She knew what different plants needed: constant moisture or summer drought, winter protection or none at all, acid soil or chalk. She knew how colors worked together, and precisely what colors her flowers would be. To a large extent, she personally built the English primrose industry by saving seedlings with good clear colors and ruthlessly weeding out those with colors that were weak or muddy. She knew, from her years as an artist, which color combinations set the teeth on edge and which enchant the eye.

This kind of knowledge only comes from long experience with many different plants grown under lots of different conditions. It helps the gardener sort out the plants that belong in the cutting garden rather than the herbaceous border, for example. Some flowers have wonderful blooms, but a deplorable tendency to get their faces dirty by lying in the mud. Some are ugly out of bloom, subject to blights, or inclined to leave huge empty places in the garden when they die back. Some are new to the garden and the gardener, and one needs a bit of experience with them to determine where they would do best. The

cutting garden functions nicely as a training ground for both the border and the gardener.

The Cutting Garden

A cutting garden need not take up vast amounts of space. A neglected side yard is a fine place to grow plants that must be staked or are unattractive out of bloom. It's a grand place to plant spring and summer bulbs so that bouquets for the house don't leave the garden looking stripped, and dying foliage doesn't spoil the looks of the garden. It's the only place to grow freesias (*Freesia*), since they will not stand up by themselves, and their sweet fragrance is not to be missed. Old-fashioned carnations or clove pinks (*Dianthus caryophyllus*), with their tendency to flop all over the place are good candidates for the cutting garden. There they can be staked and tied as much as necessary because they are not on display. (It always looks to me like some perverted version of bondage to see flowers tied to stakes.) The rich clove fragrance of carnations is a joy and a delight, and reason enough by itself to grow them, but their floppiness and susceptibility to rust and fusarium wilt make them difficult in the garden proper. The Belladonna lily is another good cutting garden flower, since it has only leaves in the winter and only blooms in August. Like the carnations, its scent is delicious; the fragrance will fill a room. Bearded irises are hybridized into more amazing colors and color combinations each year, many of which don't quite fit into most garden color schemes: tangerine, bronze, and wild bicolor combinations like orange and blue, which look smashing in arrangements and just plain weird in the garden. These, too, are best in the cutting garden.

Roses are perfect for the cutting garden where the fact that the pruned, dormant plants look mutilated does not force itself on your attention

The cutting garden is the place to plant all the flowers that will go into flower arrangements for the table, bouquets for the bedroom, and nosegays for friends.

every time you stroll through the garden. Dahlias (*Dahlia pinnata*) are good, too, especially the very tall types, such as the "dinner-plate" varieties. Most need large, sturdy stakes that are hard to hide in the garden unless the dahlias are in a thickly planted border. A striking, but rarely seen dahlia, the tree dahlia (*Dahlia imperialis*), grows every year to ten to twenty feet and looks exactly like a small, multistemmed tree. It has lovely lavender flowers, eight to ten inches in diameter, late in the fall when little else is in bloom. Frost kills it to the ground, leaving a large empty place in the garden, which is what relegates it to the cutting garden. The flowers are superb in arrangements. It is grown from cuttings rooted in sand or root clumps. (In

cold climates, lift the roots and store them at fifty degrees F in dry sand, sawdust, or vermiculite.)

Bachelor's-buttons look tatty if they're not dead-headed every five minutes. Shasta daisies (*Chrysanthemum* x *superbum*) like to sprawl. The classic white Madonna lily is susceptible to a virus that can infect other lilies. Better to plant it in the cutting garden away from the other summer lilies, and pick all you want for the house. Annual baby's breath (*Gypsophila elegans*) only lives a month or six weeks, so it must be resown on open ground once a month from spring through summer, a chore that's easier in the cutting garden than in the border.

Still, who can imagine summer without huge

blue-and-white bouquets of bachelor's-buttons, and baby's breath, vases full of sweet-smelling Madonna lilies, armfuls of Shasta daisies? It's probably illegal to have a summer house and not fill it with big bouquets. It may be illegal to have summer and not fill the house with fresh flowers.

The purpose of the cutting garden is merely to bring the flowers to bloom to be cut for the house, so one can plant any which way without feeling that one has violated the principles of good gardening. If it looks good, it's pure happenstance. That's why cutting gardens are best slipped into invisible corners or in otherwise unused side yards.

THE CHILDREN'S GARDEN

Invisible corners are also good places to put in a children's garden, because, as with the cutting garden, elegant design is not a part of the process. The purpose is to grow things, preferably fun things. Fun stuff to grow includes giant sunflowers, immense 'Big Max' Halloween pumpkins, all kinds of gourds, blue potatoes, purple yard-long beans, yellow spaghetti squash, scarlet runner beans, baby watermelons (*Citrullus lanatus*), small tomatoes ('Atom', 'Patio', 'Tiny Tim', and 'Sweet 100' are all good choices), and little round 'Butterball' carrots. For flowers, choose the brightest, easiest, and sturdiest to be found: zinnias, marigolds, nasturtiums, daisies, petunias, geraniums, and dwarf dahlias, all of which make fine bouquets for a little person's bedroom or the family dining table. Snapdragons are essential: squeezed on the sides, the flowers "talk." Old-fashioned pansies have "faces" in their flowers, and the child hasn't been born yet that doesn't love Johnny-jump-ups.

Pumpkins, gourds, giant sunflowers, beans, watermelons, and carrots are best planted from seeds. Tomatoes and flowers do best planted as seedlings. That way, there's something for the small gardener to see besides bare ground, and there's still the excitement of checking every day to see if the first sprouts are up. Remember the old rule for planting seeds: "Two for the cutworm, one for the crow, one for the beetle, and four to grow." Children's gardens need to be small—a space three feet-by-four feet will probably do the job. As in the cutting garden, don't worry about how it looks. Children have their own notions of what will go where. The idea is for the child to have fun, not to win a scholarship to the Harvard School of Landscape Design before he or she is six.

Gourds are great fun just because the shapes and colors are so strange. Rag gourds (*Luffas*) can be made into grand bath scrubs for Christmas gifts; they're not difficult to make, and cost a small fortune to buy. The pumpkin, of course, is to carve for Halloween and to make roasted pumpkin seeds. The other gourds make fine fall decorations and centerpieces. Sunflower seeds can be eaten or left for the birds, and the night navy blue mashed potatoes are served at dinner will be a banner day in the small gardener's life.

Do not plant radishes, peppers, onions, or cabbage in the children's garden. Children are born hating foods that are hot or very strongly flavored. That's why they love mashed potatoes and buttered noodles. Only adults are foolish enough to eat foods that smart or sting or stink.

Do not plant a children's garden in the hope of getting the children to eat vegetables. They won't. Don't plant vegetables your children hate. They won't like them any better for having grown them in their very own garden. Plant the garden in the hope that they will be fascinated by the process of growing things, by the wonder of seeing seeds and seedlings turn into flowers and food, by the fun of playing in the dirt. Keep clearly in mind that a children's garden is not a moral lesson in "oughts" and "shoulds" and "have tos."

Snapdragons (right) are easy to grow and fun as well. Squeeze the sides of a snapdragon to make it "talk," and your reputation with the younger set is assured.

Here is a wealth of ornamental gourds (below), complete with all their wondrous stripes and stipples and patches and patterns of color in an amazing assortment of shapes and sizes.

It is a spiritual lesson in the entwined twin miracles of life and growth.

A GARDEN OF MEMORIES

I have wanted for years to redesign my mother's garden. My mother will not hear of it. I want to plant an oleander hedge to give the backyard privacy, but it would mean taking out the immense clumps of amaryllis along the fence. "Oh, those were left by the Blakeslees when we bought the house," my mother says. That was forty-five years ago. I suggest transplanting the gazania to make room for a pretty little lawn. "Oh, Dottie gave me those gazania," my mother says. Dottie was a dear friend who died much too young. I recommend potting up some huge old geraniums to make room for a handsome redwood deck. "Oh, Flora gave me those, and they've done so well," my mother says. Flora and my mother had been friends since childhood, more than fifty years of friendship.

When I look at my mother's garden, I see plants. When my mother looks at her garden, she sees her friends. She doesn't want Dottie transplanted or Flora potted up.

Every tree, shrub, flower, even down to ground covers, comes with its own story. The Chinese elm is one of three seedlings she and my father dug from a friend's house thirty-five years ago. One was planted in back, the other two in front. When it became obvious that the two Chinese elms threatened the end of the front lawn, with roots erupting everywhere and the grass shaded out, my Grandmother Godwin took them out and traded them with a local nurseryman for two liquidambar whose roots were better behaved. In the same transaction, she brought home the lemon tree.

The jade tree plant (*Crassula argentea*) that lines the side yard came from Mrs. Myers, the elderly widow next door. It grows to an unheard-of size, and every time it gets out of bounds, my mother whacks it brutally about the head and shoulders and pokes the pieces she's whacked off in the sandy soil. They all grow just fine. Don't talk to my mother about hardening off or dusting with charcoal or dipping in Rootone™ or heeling cuttings in flats of vermiculite. Why would anyone bother when you can simply stick branches three inches in diameter in the ground and they grow? *Sunset* says that jade tree grows slowly to a height of nine feet. *Sunset* ought to talk to my mother.

The ash tree, which along with the Chinese elm has ruined the back lawn, came from the Curtises down the street. The camellia came from her friend Eloise, the oleander from Mrs. Scales across the street, and the elephants-ear (*Colocasia esculenta*) was a present from one of her classes. A pair of my father's photography students contributed the cactus; the periwinkle was a gift from a neighbor, Anne-Marie; the mother-in-law's tongue (*Sansevieria trilasciata*) was presented by a fellow professor, Doris; and my sister, Jo Beth, gave her the mums. Me? I contributed the roses.

One may move plants around pretty much as one will, but friends and memories must be respected. My mother's yard may never have the oleander hedge that would block out the view of the neighbor's yards. It will probably never have the large redwood deck that would hide the havoc wreaked by the elm and ash roots. The old patio will never be replaced with the lawn my father has talked about putting in for the past twenty years. The arbor of wisteria will never soften the lines of the garage. But the Blakeslees are remembered every time the amaryllis blooms, and Flora's friendship is in every leaf and petal of the geraniums. There are places, as in the cutting garden and the children's garden, where design and effect have nothing to do with anything. My mother's garden of memories is one of them.

SOURCES

GARDENS TO VISIT

United States

Allerton Gardens
South Coast Tropical Botanical
   Research Station
Kauai
This garden is a stunning example of what
unlimited money can accomplish given the
time, the inclination, and a magnificent setting. Bromeliads are used as bedding plants
and the koi come to a hand clap.

Arnold Arboretum
Harvard University
Cambridge, MA

Callaway Gardens
U.S. Highway 27
Pine Mountain, GA
(800) 282-8181
An extraordinary collection of native
rhododendrons and azaleas as well as
thousands of hybrids, many developed here
by Fred Galle, about 2,500 acres worth.

Descanso Gardens
Flintridge/La Canada, CA
A major camellia collection amid century-old
oaks.

Dumbarton Oaks
31st and R Streets
Washington, DC
The best Beatrix Farrand garden in America,
and arguably the finest garden on the continent. An Italian Renaissance garden by the
only female founding member of the
American Society of Landscape Architects.

Filoli
Canada Road
Woodside, CA
(415) 366-4640
Sixteen acres of formal display gardens with a
series of "garden rooms," including the Char-
tres window garden and a sunken garden,
among others. Formerly a private estate, Filoli
is now open to the public.

Foster Botanic Garden
Honolulu, Hawaii
Tropical trees and lots of bromeliads and
orchids.

Longwood Gardens
Route One South
Kennett Square, PA
(215) 388-6741
Over 1,000 acres of display gardens, 30 miles
outside Philadelphia, reflecting the influence
of both the French formal tradition and the
English parkland tradition.

Middleton Place
Charleston, SC
A magnificently romantic American garden
begun in 1741. Off the Ashley River Road on
the Ashley River a half-hour from
Charleston's Historic District.

Strybing Arboretum
Golden Gate Park
San Francisco, CA
(415) 661-1316
Excellent Mediterranean-climate collection
and California native plant collection.
Golden Gate Park also has a very good
Japanese tea garden across the street from the
arboretum, and a lovely conservatory.

The United States National Arboretum
3501 New York Avenue N.E.
Washington, DC
(202) 475-4859
A vast collection of trees and shrubs on 444
acres; in the spring, 60,000 azaleas bloom.
Superb bonsai collection with a number of
specimens more than a century old.

Canada

Allen Gardens
Toronto, Ontario
Greenhouses in the heart of town featuring
cacti and succulents, orchids, and aquatic
plants.

Bagatelle
1635 Chemin St. Louis
Sillery, Quebec
A charming small estate garden just outside
the city limits of Quebec City.

Bois de Coulonge
Quebec City, Quebec
Large collections of exotic plants.

Devonian Gardens
Calgary, Alberta
An indoor/outdoor garden in an urban setting, complete with multi-story office
buildings.

Dr. Sun Yat-Sen Garden
578 Carrall Street
Vancouver, B.C.
(604) 662-3207
A Chinese garden located in Vancouver's
Chinatown.

Halifax Public Garden
Halifax, Nova Scotia

Jardin Van Den Hend
St. Foy, Quebec
(418) 656-3410
Botanical garden with plants grouped
according to their botanical classification, a
sort of botanic family affair.

Minter Gardens
52892 Bunker Road
Rosedale, B.C.
(604) 794-7191

Montreal Botanical Garden
Montreal, Quebec
(514) 872-2429
The largest botanical garden on the North
American continent, third largest in the
world after Berlin in Germany and Kew in
England.

Muttart Conservatory
Edmonton, Alberta
Pyramidal glasshouses each representing a
particular climate zone.

Nitobe Memorial Garden
University of British Columbia
Vancouver, B.C.
(604) 228-4208
An especially fine Japanese garden with pretty
little lakes and streams, maples, azaleas, and
Japanese iris.

The Bloedel Conservatory
Queen Elizabeth Park
Vancouver, B.C.

Van Dusen Botanical Garden
37th Avenue and Oak Street
Vancouver, B.C.
(604) 266-7194

England

Blenheim Palace
Oxfordshire, England
The vast English park in all its glory. Some people think Lancelot "Capability" Brown ruined Blenheim when he turned the parterres into lawns and flooded Vanbrugh's bridge to well above its knees.

Hidcote Manor
Gloucestershire, England
A simply lovely place.

Leeds Castle
Kent, England
Another piece of pure loveliness.

Magdalen College
Oxford University
Oxfordshire, England
Humphrey Repton laid out this garden in 1801. As long as you're at Oxford, don't miss the university's botanical garden along the Thames.

Sheffield Park
Sussex, England
Lancelot "Capability" Brown (in 1776) and Humphrey Repton (in 1789) both left their mark on this garden, which was partially relandscaped by Arthur G. Soames in 1920. Superb shrubs.

Syon House
Middlesex, England
Another garden by "Capability" Brown.

Tintinhull House
Somerset, England

The Royal Horticultural Society's Garden at Wisley
Surrey, England
A wonderful garden, but the restaurant serves dismal food. Eat first, and wear comfortable walking shoes.

White Lodge
Richmond Park
Surrey, England
This is the tube stop just before Kew coming from London; park signs request that you not pet the deer during rutting season. William Kent is believed to have laid out the gardens at White Lodge between 1731 and 1735, and Humphrey Repton worked on it in 1805.

There are 13,000 gardens open-to-view in England, not counting those in Scotland, Wales, and Ireland. These are but a sampling.

Ireland

Mount Stewart
Northern Ireland

Scotland

The Royal Botanic Garden
Edinburgh, Scotland
A Reginald Farrar rock garden, extraordinary hedges, and wondrous peonies.

Spain

The Generalife
Grenada, Spain
The ultimate Moorish garden with cabbage rose blooms so big a child's face is completely obscured in bending to smell the roses.

The Royal Botanic Garden
Madrid, Spain

France

Giverny, France
French Impressionist Claude Monet's home and garden now restored to its original glory. The proper name of the house is *Le Pressoir*, but it is better known by the name of the town where it is located. This is a day trip from Paris, and not to be missed.

La Malmaison
Versailles, France
This is where Napoleon's Josephine planted all those roses painted by Redouté. The palace at Versailles with the Grand Trianon and the Petit Trianon is nearby with its classic French formal gardens.

Fontainebleau, France
Napoleon's favorite residence, complete with a 42,000-acre forest, fountains, and flowers.

Les Jardins des Plantes
Paris, France
A centuries-old botanical garden.

Tuileries Gardens
Rue de Rivoli
Paris, France
The true home of all French babies, their perambulators, and their heavily starched nannies. They bloom all year-round.

Luxembourg Gardens
Left Bank (Rive Gauche)
Paris, France

Italy

Boboli Gardens
Palazzo Pitti
Florence, Tuscany

Villa Medici
Accademia della Crusca
Castello, Tuscany
Begun in 1538 and much altered in the eighteenth century, the Villa Medici now houses the Accademia della Crusco, a famous language institute. The garden has an extraordinary *orangerie*, some 600 terra cotta pots of citrus trees, a system of fountains and water courses, and a magnificent grotto.

Villa Gamberaia
Tuscany

Japan

Katsura Imperial Villa
Katsura Shimizicho
Ukyo-ku, Kyoto
An outstanding example of a Japanese stroll garden laid out in the seventeenth century. Don't miss it. Apply for a pass at the Kyoto Imperial Household Agency; you will need your passport to pick up the pass the day before you visit. The same agency also handles passes for the gardens of the Sento Palace and Shugakuin Imperial Villa, which are well worth seeing.

Ryoanji Temple
Goryonoshitacho, Ryoanji,
Ukyo-ku, Kyoto
A fifteenth-century temple garden that features the world's most famous sand garden.

Saihoji
Kamigayacho, Matsuo,
Ukyo-ku, Kyoto
An extraordinarily beautiful stroll garden covered with moss created in 1339 by the Zen Buddhist priest Muso-Kokushi (1275–1351). Open by appointment only. Send a letter requesting permission at least five days in advance and include a reply card. The letter must state the date you wish to visit, your name, address, age, occupation, and nationality.

Koishikawa Korakuen Garden
Koraku
Bunkyo-ku, Tokyo
A seventeenth-century stroll garden showing some Chinese influence in its design.

Kiyosumi Garden
Kiyosumi
Koto-ku, Tokyo
A nineteenth-century stroll garden famous for the rocks collected from all over Japan.

Rikugien Garden
Honkomagome
Bunkyo-ku, Tokyo
An eighteenth-century stroll garden featuring a small lake with an island and a wooded hill.

Australia

The Botanic Gardens of Adelaide
Veale Garden on South Terrace
Himeji Japanese Garden on
    South Terrace
The Botanical Garden on North Terrace
Southern Australia
Sixteen hectares of landscaped grounds, including a conservatory, featuring native and exotic plants in the botanical garden; the other gardens are on separate grounds. All are located in the Parklands, a green belt that encircles the city of Adelaide. Wear comfortable walking shoes; this is less a garden stroll than a trek.

The Botanic Garden
The Domain
Hobart, Tasmania
Established in 1818, this garden has an interesting collection of both native and exotic plants.

The Royal Botanic Garden
Domain Road next to King's Domain
Melbourne
A superb collection of Australian native plants, as well as exotics like azaleas.

Fitzroy Gardens
Spring Street at Wellington Parade
Melbourne
Captain Cook's stone cottage was brought from England and re-erected here to honor the first Englishman to lay eyes on what is either the world's largest island or the world's smallest continent. There is a conservatory in addition to the outdoor plantings.

King's Park
Central Perth
West Australia
Blanketed with native wildflowers in September and October; essentially a wild garden on the edge of Perth.

South Africa

Kirstenbosch Botanical Garden
Capetown, South Africa
The world's finest collection of the extraordinary Cape flora as well as an excellent collection of specimens from the Karoo. Not to be missed on any account.

ANNUALS

Applewood Seed Co.
Box 10761, Edgemont Station
Golden, CO 80401

W. Atlee Burpee
300 Park Ave.
Warminster, PA 18974

Comstock Ferre & Co.
263 Main St.
Wethersfield, CT 06109

Dominion Seed House
115 Guelph St.
Georgetown, Ontario
Canada L7G 4A2

Henry Field Seed Co.
407 Sycamore St.
Shenandoah, IA 51602

Gurney Seed & Nursery Co.
Yankton, SD 57079

Joseph Harris Co.
Moreton Farm
Rochester, NY 14624

The Charles Hart Seed Co.
Main & Hart Streets
Wethersfield, CT 06109

H.G. Hastings Co.
Box 4274
Atlanta, GA 30302

J.L. Hudson, Seedsman
Box 1058
Redwood City, CA 94064

Johnny's Selected Seeds
Albion, ME 04910

J.W. Jung Seed Co.
Randolph, WI 53956

Laval Seeds Inc.
3505 Boul St. Martin
Chomedey Laval
Quebec, Canada H7V 2T3

Orol Ledden & Sons
Center St.
Sewell, NJ 08080

Earl May Seed & Nursery Co.
Box 500
Shenandoah, IA 51603

McLaughlin's Seeds
Box 550
Mead, WA 99021

Mellinger's Inc.
North Lima, OH 44452

Nichol's Herbs & Rare Seeds
1190 N. Pacific Hwy.
Albany, OR 97321

L.L. Olds Seed Co.
2901 Packers Ave.
Madison, WI 53707

George W. Park Seed Co.
Box 31
Greenwood, SC 29647

W.H. Perron & Co. Ltd.
515 Labelle Blvd.
Chomedey Laval
Quebec, Canada H7V 2T3

Plants of the Southwest
1812 Second St.
Santa Fe, NM 87501

Clyde Robin Seed Co.
Box 2366
Castro Valley, CA 94546

Stokes Seed Inc.
Box 548
Buffalo, NY 14240

Thompson & Morgan
Box 1308
Jackson, NJ 08527

Otis S. Twilley Seed Co.
Box 65
Trevose, PA 19047

PERENNIALS

Andre Viette Nursery
Route 1, Box 16
Fisherville, VA 22939

Bluestone Perennials
7211 Middle Ridge Rd.
Madison, OH 44057

Busse Gardens
Rt. 2, Box 13
635 E. Seventh St.
Cokato, MN 55321

Canyon Creek Nursery
3527 Dry Creek Rd.
Oroville, CA 95965

Caprice Farm Nursery
15425 S.W. Pleasant Hill Rd.
Sherwood, OR 97140

Carman's Nursery
18201 SW Mozart Ave.
Los Gatos, CA 95030

Carroll Gardens
Box 310
Westminster, MD 21157

Country Hills Greenhouse
Rt. 2
Corning, OH 43730

Crownsville Nursery
Box 797
Crownsville, MD 21032

C.A. Cruickshank, Ltd.
1015 Mt. Pleasant Rd.
Toronto, ON, Canada
M4P 2MI

Eco-Gardens
Box 1227
Decatur, GA 30031
rock garden plants

Englerth Gardens
Rt. 2
22461 Twenty-Second St.
Hopkins, MI 49328

Garden Place
6780 Heisley Rd.
Box 388
Mentor, OH 44061-0388

Gilson Gardens
Box 227
Perry, OH 44081

Heaths & Heathers
Box 850
Elma, WA 98541

Holbrook Farm & Nursery
Route 2, Box 223B
Fletcher, NC 28732

Lilypons Water Gardens
6885 Lilypons Rd.
Box 10
Lilypons, MD 21717

Maver
Box 18754
Seattle, WA 98118

Mileager's Gardens
4838 Douglas Ave.
Racine, WI 53402

Prairie Nursery
Box 365
Westfield, WI 53964

Putney Nursery Inc.
Rt. 5
Putney, VT 05346

Rakestraw's Perennial Gardens
3094 S. Term St.
Burton, MI 48529

Rocknoll Nursery
9210 U.S. 50
Hillsboro, OH 45133

Savory Farms
Rt. 2, Box 753
Donalds, SC 29638

Springbrook Gardens
6776 Heisley Rd.
P.O. Box 388
Mentor, OH 44061

Stallings Nursery
910 Encinitas Blvd.
Encinitas, CA 92024

Sweet Springs Perennial Growers
2065 Ferndale Rd.
Arroyo Grande, CA 93420
Send SASE for catalog

Western Hills Nursery
16250 Coleman Valley Rd.
Occidental, CA 95465

Wildwood Farm
10300 Highway 12
Kenwood, CA 95452

Wildflower Seed Co.
Box 406
St. Helena, CA 94574

Yerba Buena Nursery
19500 Skyline Blvd.
Woodside, CA 94062

BULBS

American Daylily & Perennials
Box 7008
The Woodlands, TX 77380

Amaryllis Inc.
Box 318
Baton Rouge, LA 78021

Antonelli Brothers
2545 Capitol Rd.
Santa Cruz, CA 95062
begonias

Bakker of Holland
Box 50
Louisiana, MO 63353
Catalog free

Blue Dahlia Gardens
Box 316
San Jose, IL 62682
Catalog free

Brecks
Box 1757
Peoria, IL 61656

Comanche Acres Iris Gardens
Box 258
Gower, MO 64454
Catalog $1.00

Connell's Dahlias
10216 40th Ave.
Tacoma, WA 98446

Cooley's Gardens
Box 126
11553 Silverton Rd., NE
Silverton, OR 97381
Catalog $2.00

C.A. Cruickshank, Ltd.
1015 Mt. Pleasant Rd.
Toronto, ON, Canada
M4P 2MI
Catalog $2.00

The Daffodil Mart
Box 794
Gloucester, VA 23061
Catalog free

Dahlias by Phil Traff
1316 132nd Ave.
Summer, WA 98390

Daylily World
Box 1612
Sanford, FL 32771

Peter De Jaeger Bulb Co.
Box 2010
South Hamilton, MA 01982
Catalog free

Dutch Gardens
Box 200
Adelphia, NJ 07710
Catalog $1.00

Fairyland Begonia Garden
1100 Griffith Rd.
McKinleyville, CA 95521
begonias

Flad's Glads
2109 Cliff Ct.
Madison, WI 53713
gladiolus

French Irish Gardens
621 S. 3rd Ave.
Walla Walla, WA 99362
Catalog $2.00

Garden of the Enchanted Rainbow
Box 439
Killeen, AL 35645
Catalog $1.00

Gladside Gardens
61 Main St.
Northfield, MA 01360
gladiolus

Grant Mitsch Novelty Daffodils
Box 218
Hubbard, OR 97032
Catalog $3.00

Greenwood Nursery
Box 1610
Goleta, CA 93116
Catalog $3.00

Gurney Seed & Nursery
Second & Capital Streets
Yankton, SD 57078
Catalog free

Robert B. Hamm
Box 160903
Sacramento, CA 95816-0903
begonias

Holly Haven
136 Sanwood Rd.
Knoxville, TN 37923

Hollyland U.S.A.
Box 754
Millville, NJ 08332

International Growers Exchange
Box 52248
Livonia, MI 48152
Catalog $5.00

Iris Country
Roger Nelson
118 Lincoln St.
Wayne, NE 68787

J.W. Jung Co.
335 S. High St.
Randolph, WI 53957
Catalog free

Kartuz Greenhouses
1408 Sunset Dr.
Vista, CA 92083
begonias

Klehm Nursery
Box 197
South Barrington, IL 60010
Catalog $2.00

Legg Dahlia Gardens
1069 Hastings Rd.
Geneva, NY 14456

Earl May Nursery Co.
Box 500
Shenandoah, IA 51603
Catalog free

Maple Tree Gardens
Box 278
Ponca, NE 68770
Catalog free

Maryott's Iris Garden
1073 Bird Ave.
San Jose, CA 95125

McMillens Iris Garden
R.R. #1
Norwich, ONT Canada, N0J 1P0
Catalog free

Messelaar Bulb Co.
Box 269
Ipswich, MA 01938

Michigan Bulb Co.
1950 Waldorf NW
Grand Rapids, MI 49550
Catalog free

Mid-America Iris Garden
Box 12982
Oklahoma City, OK 73157

Charles H. Mueller
River Rd.
New Hope, PA 18938
Catalog free

Oakwood Daffodils
2330 W. Bertrand Rd.
Niles, MI 49120
Catalog free

Oregon Bulb Farms
14071 N.E. Arndt Rd.
Aurora, OR 97002
lilies

George W. Park Seed Co.
Box 31
Greenwood, SC 29648
Catalog free

Pinetree Garden Seeds
Rte. 100N
Gloucester, ME 04260
Catalog free

Rex Bulb Farms
Box 774
Port Townsend, WA 98368
lilies

John Scheepers Inc.
63 Wall St.
New York, NY 10005
Catalog free

Smith & Hawken
25 Corte Madera Ave.
Mill Valley, CA 94941
Catalog free

Swan Island Dahlias
Box 800
Canby, OR 97013

Ty Ty Plantation
Box 159
Ty Ty, GA 31795
Catalog free

K. Van Bourgondien & Sons, Inc.
Box A
Babylon, NY 11702
Catalog free

Van Engelen, Inc.
307 Maple St.
Litchfield, CT 06759
Catalog free

Veldheer Tulip Gardens
12755 Quincy St.
Holland, MI 49424

Waushara Gardens
Box 570
Plainsfield, WI 54966

White Flower Farm
Rte. 63
Litchfield, CT 06759
Catalog $5.00

Gilbert H. Wild & Son, Inc.
Box 338
1112 Joplin Street
Sarcoxie, MO 64862
Catalog $2.00

ROSES

Antique Rose Emporium
Route 5, Box 143
Brenham, TX 77833

Armstrong Roses
P.O. Box 1020
Somis, CA 93066
Catalog free

BDK Nursery
P.O. Box 628
2091 Haas Rd.
Apopka, FL 32712
Catalog free

Fred Edmunds Roses
6235 SW Kahle Rd.
Wilsonville, OR 97070

Emlong Nurseries
2671 W. Marquette Woods Rd.
Stevensville, MI 49127
Catalog free

Greenmantle Nursery
3010 Ettersburg Rd.
Garberville, CA 95440
antique roses

Gurney Seed & Nursery Co.
2nd & Capital
Yankton, SD 57078
Catalog free

Hastings
P.O. Box 4274
Atlanta, Ga 30302-4274
Catalog free

Heritage Rosarium
211 Haviland Mill Rd.
Brookville, MD 20833

Heritage Rose Gardens
16831 Mitchell Creek Dr.
Ft. Bragg, CA 95437

High Country Rosarium
1717 Downing St.
Denver, CO 80218
antique roses

Historical Roses
1657 W. Jackson St.
Painesville, OH 44077

Hortico, Inc.
723 Robson Rd., R.R.1
Waterdown, ON, Canada L0R 2H0

Jackson & Perkins Co.
P.O. Box 1028
Medford, OR 97501
Catalog free

Justice Miniature Roses
5947 S.W. Kahle Rd.
Wilsonville, OR 97070

Krider Nurseries
P.O. Box 29
Middlebury, IN 46540
Catalog free

Lowe's Own-Root Roses
6 Sheffield Rd.
Nashua, NH 03062
antique roses

MB Farm Miniature Roses
Jamison Hill Rd.
Clinton Corners, NY 12514

McConnell Nurseries, Inc.
R.R.1
Port Burwell, ON, Canada N0J 1T0

McDaniel's Miniature Roses
7523 Zemco St.
Lemon Grove, CA 92045

Milaeger's Gardens
4838 Douglas Ave.
Racine, WI 53402-2498

Mini-Roses
P.O. Box 4255, Sta. A
Dallas, TX 75208

Miniature Plant Kingdom
4125 Harrison Grade Rd.
Sebastopol, CA 95472

Moore Miniature Roses
2519 Visalia Ave.
Visalia, CA 93277

Nor' East Miniature Roses
58 Hammond St.
Rowley, MA 01969

Pickering Nurseries Inc.
670 Kingston Rd. (Hwy. 2)
Pickering, ON, Canada L1V 1A6
antique roses

Pixie Treasures Miniature Rose Nursery
4121 Prospect Ave.
Yorba Linda, CA 92686

Rose Acres
6641 Crystal Blvd.
Diamond Springs, CA 95619

The Rose Garden & Mini Rose Nursery
P.O. Box 560
SC Highway 560 (Austin Street)
Cross Hill, SC 29332-0560

Roses by Fred Edmunds
6235 S.W. Kahle Rd.
Wilsonville, OR 97070
Catalog free

Roses of Yesterday & Today
802 Brown's Valley Rd.
Watsonville, CA 95076-0398

Rosehill Farm
Gregg Neck Rd.
Galena, MD 21635

Savage Farms Nursery
P.O. Box 125
Highway 56 South
McMinnville, TN 37110
Catalog free

Spring Hill Nurseries Co.
P.O. Box 1758
Peoria, IL 61656
Catalog free

Stark Brothers Nurseries & Orchard Co.
Highway 54 West
Louisiana, MO 63353-0010
Catalog free

Thomasville Nurseries
P.O. Box 7
1842 Smith Ave.
Thomasville, GA 31799-0007

Tiny Petals Nursery
489 Minot Ave.
Chula Vista, CA 92010

Wayside Gardens
P.O. Box 1
Hodges, SC 29695-0001
Catalog $1.00

TREES AND SHRUBS

Beaver Creek Nursery
7526 Pelleaux Rd.
Knoxville, TN 37938
Specializes in collector's trees
and shrubs.
Catalog $1.00

The Bovees Nursery
1737 S.W. Coronado
Portland, OR 97219
Specializes in species and hybrid
rhododendrons.
Catalog $2.00

W. Atlee Burpee Co.
300 Park Ave.
Warminster, PA 18974
Offers plants, seeds, books, supplies, tools,
and bulbs.
Catalog free

Cardinal Nursery
Rt. 1, Box 97
State Road, NC 28676

Carroll Gardens
P.O. Box 310
444 East Main St.
Westminster, MD 21157
Large selection including hollies,
yews, viburnums, and much more.
Catalog $2.00

Cummins Garden
22 Robertsville Rd.
Marlboro, NJ 07746
evergreens and miscellany

Gardens of the Blue Ridge
P.O. Box 10
U.S. 221 N.
Pineola, NC 28662
Good selection of native shrubs.
Catalog $2.00

Girard Nurseries
P.O. Box 428
6801 North Ridge (US 20)
Geneva, OH 44041
Broad selection of flowering shrubs, dwarf
conifers, rhododendrons, azaleas, and hollies.
Catalog free

Gurney Seed & Nursery Co.
2nd and Capital
Yankton, SC 57078
Offers broad selection of plants
and seeds.
Catalog free

Hall Rhododendrons
1280 Quince Dr.
Junction City, OR 97448
Offers broad selection of species and hybrid
rhododendrons and azaleas.
Catalog $1.00

Hortico, Inc.
723 Robson Rd., R.R.1
Waterdown, ON, Canada L0R 2H0
Specializes in a broad selection of garden
perennials along with ornamental trees,
shrubs, ferns, wildflowers, and conifers.
Catalog free

Krider Nurseries
P.O. Box 29
Middlebury, IN 46540
Broad selection of fruit trees, berries,
ornamental trees, shrubs, and roses.
Catalog free

Lawyer Nursery, Inc.
950 Highway 200 West
Plains, MT 59859
Many types of ornamental trees, fruit and nut
trees, rootstock for fruit trees, conifers, and
shrubs.
Catalog free

Musser Forests, Inc.
P.O. Box 340
Route 119 North
Indiana, PA 15710-0340
Supplies trees, shrubs, and
ground covers.
Catalog free

Spring Hill Nurseries Co.
P.O. Box 1758
Peoria, IL 61656
Broad selection of perennials, flowering
shrubs, ground covers.
Catalog free

Wayside Gardens
P.O. Box 1
Hodges, SC 29695-0001
Offers ornamental trees and shrubs.
Catalog $1.00

Westgate Garden Nursery
751 Westgate Dr.
Eureka, CA 95501

Winterset Nursery
R.D. 3, Box 58
Kring St.
St. Johnstown, PA 15004
hardy rhododendrons

HERBS

Abundant Life Seed Foundation
Box 771
1029 Lawrence
Port Townsend, WA 98368
Offers a wide selection of herb seeds.
Catalog $1.00

W. Atlee Burpee Co.
300 Park Ave.
Warminster, PA 18974
Offers both herb seeds and plants.
Catalog free

C.A. Cruickshank, Ltd.
1015 Mt. Pleasant Rd.
Toronto, ON, Canada M4P 2MI
Catalog $2.00

Caprilands Herb Farm
Silver St.
North Coventry, CT 06238
Offers herb plants. Display gardens open to
the public.

Carroll Gardens
Box 310
Westminster, MD 21157
Offers perennial herb plants.
Catalog $2.00

Comstock, Ferre & Company
Box 125
Wethersfield, CT 06109
Offers herb seeds.
Catalog free

The Cook's Garden
Box 65
Moffits Bridge
Londonderry, VT 05148
Offers an extensive selection of herbs.
Catalog $1.00

Fox Hill Farm
440 West Michigan Ave.
Parma, MI 49269
Offers 350 varieties of herbs and
scented geraniums.
Catalog $1.00

Le Jardin du Gourmet
Box 44 West
Danville, VT 05873-0044
Features packets of herb seed at low cost.
Catalog 50¢

Nichols Garden Nursery
1190 North Pacific Hwy.
Albany, OR 97321
Offers herbs to grow from seed.
Catalog free

Geo. W. Park Seed Co.
Box 31
398 Cokesbury Rd.
Greenwood, SC 29647
Features herbs to grow from seed.
Catalog free

Pinetree Garden Seeds
Route 100 North
New Gloucester, ME 04260
Features many herbs to grow from seed.
Catalog free

Redwood City Seed Co.
Box 361
Redwood City, CA 94064
Offers herbs to grow from seed.
Catalog 50¢

Roses of Yesterday & Today
802 Brown's Valley Rd.
Watsonville, CA 95076
Offers fragrant and old-fashioned roses for
potpourri.
Catalog $1.00

Thompson & Morgan
Box 1308
Jackson, NJ 08527
Offers herb seeds.
Catalog free

Well-Sweep Herb Farm
317 Mt. Bethel Rd.
Port Murray, NJ 07865
Offers herb plants. Display gardens
open to the public.
Catalog $1.00

ORNAMENTAL GRASS PLANTS AND SEEDS, BAMBOO

Abundant Life Seed Foundation
P.O. Box 7721
Port Townsend, WA 98368

American Bamboo Co.
345 W. 2nd St.
Dayton, OH 45402
Hardy bamboo

W. Atlee Burpee Co.
300 Park Ave.
Warminster, PA 18974

Babikow Greenhouses
7838 Babikow Rd.
Baltimore, MD 21237

Bamboo Sourcery
Gerald Bol
666 Wagnon Rd.
Sebastopol, CA 95472

Kurt Bluemel, Inc.
2740 Greene Ln.
Baldwin, MD 21013

Coastal Garden & Nursery
46111 Socastee Blvd.
Myrtle Beach, SC 29575

Ernst Crownvetch Farms
R.D. 5
Meadville, PA 16335
Seeds and plants for reclamation
and conservation plantings

Goble Seed Co.
P.O. Box 203
Gunnison, UT 84634
Native grass seeds, plants

John Greenlee & Assoc.
301 E. Franklin Ave.
Pomona, CA 91766

High Altitude Gardens
P.O. Box 4238
Ketchum, ID 83340

Lafayette Home Nursery, Inc.
R.R. 1, Box 1-A
Lafayette, IL 61449
Plants and seeds

Larner Seeds
P.O. Box 407
Bolinas, Ca 94924

Limerock Ornamental Grasses
R.D. 1, Box 111-C
Port Matilda, PA 16870

Lofts Seed, Inc.
P.O. Box 146
Bound Brook, NJ 08805
Native grass seed, wildflower seeds,
and mixtures

Milaeger's Gardens
4838 Douglas Ave.
Racine, WI 53402-2498
Native and ornamental grasses

Miller Grass Seed Co., Inc.
P.O. Box 886
Hereford, TX 79045
Native grasses and wildflowers, seeds

Native Gardens
Rte. 1, Box 494
Greenback, TN 37742

Neiman Environments Nursery
2701 Cross Timbers
Flower Mound, TX 75028

Niche Gardens
Rte. 1, Box 290
Chapel Hill, NC 27516

Northplain Seed Producers
P.O. Box 9107
Moscow, ID 83843
Range and reclamation grasses,
many natives

Norwood Farms
P.O. Drawer 438
McBee, SC 29101

George W. Park Seed Co.
Box 31
Greenwood, SC 29647-0001

Plants of the Wild
Box 866
Tekoa, WA 99033

Prairie Moon Nursery
Rte. 3, Box 163
Winona, MN 55987

Prairie Ridge Nursery
R.R. 2
9738 Overland Rd.
Mount Horeb, WI 53572-2832
Native grasses, consulting and planning
service specializing in restoring and recon-
structing native ecosystems, especially
prairies and wetlands

Steve Ray's Bamboo Gardens
909 79th Pl. South
Birmingham, AL 35206

Stock Seed Farms, Inc.
Rte 1, Box 112
Murdock, NE 68407
Native grass seed

Thompson & Morgan
P.O. Box 1308
Jackson, NJ 08627
Annual and perennial grass seed

Triple Brook Farm
37 Middle Rd.
Southampton, MA 01073

Andre Viette Farm & Nursery
Rte. 1, Box 16
Fishersville, VA 22939

Wildflowers from Natures Way
R.R. 1, Box 62
Woodburn, IA 50275
Native grass seeds and plants, consulting

Winterfield Ranch Seed
Box 97
Swan Valley, ID 83449
High-altitude, cool-season native grasses

FRUITS AND VEGETABLES

Alberta Nurseries & Seeds
Bowden, Alberta
Canada TOM OKO

Archias' Seed Store
P.O. Box 109
Sedalia, MO 65301

Burrell's
Rocky Ford, CO 81067
Large selection of melons

Burgess Seed & Plant Co.
905 Four Seasons Rd.
Bloomington, IL 61701

W. Atlee Burpee Co.
300 Park Ave.
Warminster, PA 18974

Comstock Ferre & Co.
Box 125
Wethersfield, CT 06109

William Dam Seeds
P.O. Box 8400
Dundas, Ontario
Canada L9H 6M1

De Giorgi Co.
P.O. Box 413
Council Bluffs, IA 51502

Early's Farm & Garden Center
Box 3024
Saskatoon, Saskatchewan
Canada S7K 3S9

Farmer Seed & Nursery
818 NW 4th St.
Faribault, MN 55021

Henry Field Seed & Nursery
407 Sycamore St.
Shenandoah, IA 51602

Garden Magic
P.O. Box 6570
Zephyr Cove, NV 89449

Gardenimport
P.O. Box 760
Thornhill, Ontario
Canada L3T 4A5
North American supplier for Suttons,
an English seed company

Gurney's
Yankton, SD 57079

Harris Seeds
Moreton Farm
Rochester, NY 14624

Hastings
P.O. Box 4274
Atlanta, GA 30302
Many southern varieties

Ed Hume Seeds
P.O. Box 1450
Kent, WA 98032

Island Seed Co.
P.O. Box 4278, Sta. A
Victoria, British Columbia
Canada V8X 3X8

Johnny's Selected Seeds
Albion, ME 04910

Jung Seed Co.
Randolph, WI 53957

Lagomarsino Seeds
5675-A Power Inn Dr.
Sacramento, CA 95824

Landreth's Seeds
180-188 West Ostend St.
Baltimore, MD 21230

Ledden & Sons
P.O. Box 7
Sewell, NJ 08080

Letherman's Seeds
1221 Tuscarawas St.
Canton, OH 44707

Liberty Seed Co.
P.O. Box 806
New Philadelphia, OH 44663

Lindenberg Seeds
803 Princess Ave.
Brandon, Manitoba
Canada R7A OP5

Lockhart Seeds
P.O. Box 1361
Stockton, CA 95205
Extensive selection of hybrids

Earl May Nursery Co.
Box 500
Shenandoah, IA 51603

McFayden Seed Co.
P.O. Box 1800
Brandon, Manitoba
Canada R7A 6N4

Meyer Seed Co.
600 S. Caroline St.
Baltimore, MD 21231

The Natural Gardening Co.
217 San Anselmo Ave.
San Anselmo, CA 94960
Only organic mail-order nursery in U.S.

Olds Seed Co.
P.O. Box 7790
Madison, WI 53707
Several varieties not available elsewhere

Srokes Seeds
Box 548
Buffalo, NY 14240
Large selection of varieties for
short seasons

T & T Seeds, Inc.
Box 338
Grand Forks, ND 58206

T & T Seeds, Ltd.
P.O. Box 1710
Winnipeg, Manitoba
Canada R3C 3P6

Tait & Sons
P.O. Box 2873
Norfolk, VA 23504

Twilley Seed Co.
Trevose, PA 19047

Vesey's Seed
York, Prince Edward Island
Canada COA 1PO

Ontario Seed Co.
Box 144
Waterloo, Ontario
Canada N2J 3Z9

George W. Park Seed Co.
P.O. Box 31
Greenwood, SC 29646

Rawlinson Garden Seed
269 College Rd.
Truro, Nova Scotia
Canada B2N 2P6

Rohrer's
P.O. Box 25
Smoketown, PA 17576

Seedway, Inc.
Hall, NY 14463

Shepherd's Garden Seeds
30 Irene St.
Torrington, CT 06790

TOOLS AND EQUIPMENT

Ben Meadow Co.
P.O. Box 80549
3589 Broad St.
Chamblee, GA 30366

The Clapper Co.
1121 Washington St.
West Newton, MA 02165

Florist Products Inc.
2242 N. Palmer Dr.
Schaumburg, IL 60195-3883

Gardener's Eden
Box 7307
San Francisco, CA 94120-7307

Gardener's Supply
128 Intervale Rd.
Burlington, VT 05401

Kinsman Co.
River Rd.
Point Pleasant, PA 18950

A.M. Leonard, Inc.
Piqua, OH 45356

Meridan Equipment Corp.
4-40 Banta Place
Fair Lawn, NJ 07410

Modern Homesteader
921 Big Horn Ave.
Cody, WY 82414

Smith & Hawken
25 Corte Madera Ave.
Mill Valley, CA 94941

Walter F. Nick
Box 667G
Hudson, NY 12534

BIBLIOGRAPHY

Agnelli, Marella. *Gardens of the Italian Villas*. New York: Rizzoli
    Publications, 1987.

Angier, Belle Sumner. *The Garden Book of California*. New York:
    Paul Elder and Company, 1906.

Bailey, Lee. *Lee Bailey's Country Flowers*. New York: Clarkson N.
    Potter, 1985.

Baker, Richard St. Barbe. *Green Glory: The Forest of the World*.
    New York: A.A. Wyn, Incorporated, 1949.

Barber, Peter, and Phillips, C.E. Lucas. *The Trees Around Us*. Chicago:
    Follett Publishing Company, 1975.

Barton, Barbara. *Gardening by Mail*. San Francisco: Tusker Press, 1986.

Burnett, Frances Hodgson. *The Secret Garden*. New York: Lippincott,
    1938.

Clarke, Charlotte Bringle. *Edible and Useful Plants of California*.
    Berkeley: University of California Press, 1977.

Coats, Peter. *Flowers in History*. New York: Viking Press, 1970.

Colborn, Nigel. *Leisurely Gardening*. London: Christopher Helm,
    1989.

Creasy, Rosalind. *Earthly Delights*. Covelo, CA: Yolla Bolly Press
    (A Sierra Club Book), 1985.

Cruso, Thalassa. *Making Things Grow*. New York: Alfred A. Knopf,
    1972.

Doty, Walter, ed. *All About Vegetables*. San Francisco: Ortho Books,
    1973.

Earle, Alice Morse. *Old Time Gardens*. New York: Macmillan, 1901.

Engle, David H. *Japanese Gardens for Today*. Rutland, VT: Charles E. Tuttle Company, 1959.

Farrar, Reginald. *The English Rock Garden* (2 vols.). London: T.C. & E.C. Jack, Ltd., 1919.

Ferris, Roxana S. *Flowers of Point Reyes National Seashore*. Berkeley: University of California Press, 1970.

Fleming, Laurence and Gore, Alan. *The English Garden*. London: Michael Joseph, 1979.

———. *Gardening: The Complete Guide to Growing America's Favorite Fruits & Vegetables*. Massachusetts: Addison-Wesley Publishing Company, 1986.

Gerard, John. *Gerards's Herbal* (A re-issue of a book first published in 1636). New York: Crescent Books, 1985.

Hadfield, Miles. *Topiary and Ornamental Hedges*. London: Adam & Charles Black, 1971.

Hériteau, Jacqueline. *The National Arboretum Book of Outstanding Garden Plants*. New York: Simon and Schuster, 1990.

Ishimoto, Tatsuo. *The Art of the Japanese Garden*. New York: Crown Publishers, 1961.

Jekyll, Gertrude. *Wall and Water Gardens* (reprint). Salem, NH: Merrimack Publishing Circle, 1982.

———. (edited by Penelope Hobhouse) *Gertrude Jekyll on Gardening*. New York: Random House, 1985.

Johnson, Hugh. *The Principles of Gardening*. New York: Simon and Schuster, 1979.

———. *The International Book of Trees*. New York: Simon and Schuster, 1973.

Li, Hui-Lin. *The Origin and Cultivation of Shade and Ornamental Trees*. Philadelphia: University of Pennsylvania Press, 1963.

Macoboy, Stirling. *What Flower is That?* New York: Paul Hamlyn, 1973.

Mathias, Mildred E. *Color for the Landscape: Flowering Plants for Subtropical Climates*. Arcadia, CA: California Arboretum Foundation, 1976.

McLaren, John. *Gardening in California*. San Francisco: A.M. Robertson, 1909.

Midda, Sara. *In and Out of the Garden*. New York: Workman Publishing, 1981.

Munz, Philip A. *California Desert Wildflowers*. Berkeley: University of California Press, 1962.

Northern, Rebecca Tyson. *Home Orchid Growing* (3rd ed.). New York: Van Nostrand Reinhold Co., 1970.

Ortho Books, Chevron Chemical Company Editorial Staff. *All About Ground Covers*. San Francisco: Ortho Books, 1976.

———. *All About Roses*. San Francisco: Ortho Books, 1976.

———. *The World of Cactus and Succulents*. San Francisco: Ortho Books, 1977.

———. *The World of Trees*. San Francisco, Ortho Books, 1977.

Osler, Mirabel. *A Gentle Plea for Chaos*. New York: Simon and Schuster, 1989.

Otteson, Carole. *Ornamental Grasses: The Amber Wave*. New York: McGraw-Hill, 1989.

Pavel, Margaret Brandstrom. *Gardening with Color: Ideas for Planting with Annuals, Perennials, and Bulbs*. San Francisco: Ortho Books, 1977.

Ray, Richard and MacCaskey, Michael. *Roses: How to Select, Grow, and Enjoy*. Tucson, AZ: Horticultural Publishing, 1981.

Ray, Richard and Walheim, Lance. *Citrus: How to Select, Grow, and Enjoy*. Tucson, AZ: Horticultural Publishing, 1980.

Rickett, Harold William. *Wild Flowers of the United States* (6 vols.). New York: McGraw-Hill Book Company Publishers, 1966-70.

———. *Wild Flowers of America*. New York: Crown Publishers, 1969.

Riker, Tom and Rottenberg, Harvey. *The Gardener's Catalogue*. New York: William Morrow, 1974.

Rix, Martyn and Phillips, Roger. *The Bulb Book: A Photographic Guide to Over 800 Hardy Bulbs*. London: Pan Books, 1981.

Robinson, William. *The Wild Garden* (revised ed.) London: Century Publishing, 1983.

Sackville-West, Vita. *A Joy of Gardening*. New York: Harper Brothers, 1958.

———. *Vita Sackville-West's Garden Book*. New York: Atheneum, 1968.

Seike, Kiyoshi and Kudo, Masanobu with David H. Engle (ed.). *A Japanese Touch For Your Garden*. San Francisco: Kodanasha International, 1980.

Smith, Gladys. *Flowers and Ferns of Muir Woods*. Mill Valley, CA: Muir Woods Natural History Association, 1963.

Stout, Ruth and Clemence, Richard. *The Ruth Stout No-Work Garden Book*. Emmaus, PA: Rodale Press, 1973.

Stowell, Jerald P. *Bonsai: Indoors and Out*. New York: Van Nostrand Reinhold, 1966.

Sunset Books editorial staff. *Sunset New Western Garden Book*. Menlo Park, CA: Lane Publishing Company, 1983.

Tanner, Ogden. *Gardening America: Regional and Historical Influences in the Contemporary Garden*. New York: Viking Penguin, 1990.

Taylor, Ronald J. *Rocky Mountain Wildflowers*. Seattle, WA: The Mountaineers, 1982.

Thorpe, Patricia. *The American Weekend Gardener*. New York: Random House, 1988.

Tolley, Emelie and Mead, Chris. *Herbs: Gardens, Decorations, and Recipes*. New York: Clarkson N. Potter, 1985.

Vilmorin-Andrieux, MM. *The Vegetable Garden* (reprinted 1976). Palo Alto, CA: Jeavons-Leler Press, 1885.

Von Miklos, Josephine and Fire, Evelyn. *The Gardener's World*. New York: Random House, 1968.

White Katherine Sergeant. *Onward and Upward in the Garden*. New York: Farrar, Straus, Giroux, 1979.

INDEX

Page numbers in italics refer to captions and illustrations

Aconite, *136*
African marigold, *109*
Algerian ivy, *51*
Allium triquetum, 51, 55
American bittersweet, *80*
American holly, *119*
Apple tree, *112*
Appropriate gardening, 129–39
Arbors, 38–39
Archangel, *52*
Asparagus, *115*
Azaleas, *58, 61, 101*

B

Balconies
  gardens for, 148–50
  vines for, 72–74
Bamboo, *163*
  as privacy hedge, *14*, 14–15
Bartram, John, 108, 144
Bartram, William, 108, 144
Basil, *124, 151*
Beans, scarlet runner, *75, 153*
Bearded iris, *114*
Birch trees, 40, 42
Birds, 22
  feeders, 23, 25
  in meadow gardens, 143–44
  vines to attract, 78–81
  water for, *168*

Bittersweet, *80*
Black-eyed Susans, *133, 138*
Black Stallion, The (Farley), 49
Bluebonnets, *134*
Bog gardens, 39
Boston ivy, *68*
Bougainvillea, hedges, *15*
Boxwood hedge, *52*
Brown, Lancelot, 29, 30
Buildings, vines' effect on, 67–70
Bulbs, *43*
Burnett, Frances Hodgson, 49

C

California
  gardening tradition in, 36–39
  horticultural climate in, 50
  post-war suburban
    development in, 127–28
California holly, *101*
California pepper tree, *34*
Calla lily, *57, 104*
Cardinal flower, *115, 132*
Carmel Mission (California), *33*
Carpet bedding, 30–31
Catalogs, 169
Caterpillars, 23–24
Cathey, Marc, 96
Cécile Brunner rose, 60–62
Chambers, William, 108
Cherry trees, *29*, 42
Children's gardens, 174–76
Chores, minimization of, 167–68
Church, Thomas, 37
Cities
  balcony gardens for, 148–50
  cottage gardens in, 113–16
  herb and vegetable growing in,
    150–54

trees for, 118–19
  vines appropriate for, 65–67
  water supply for, 129
Citrus trees, growth in pots of,
    154–55
Clematis, *74, 81, 86, 93*
Climbing Blaze rose, *82*
Cold climate, house plants for, 104
Color, 101–2
Compost, 168
Coneflower, *132*
Containers, 67, *148*
Cook, James, 27–29
Cottage gardens, 30–31, 38
  color schemes for, *122*
  easy-to-grow plants for, 119–23
  fruit grown in, 113
  hardy plants for, 117–19
  herbs in, 123–25
  order in, 125
  as poetic gardens, 110–13
  trees in, 116
  for urban areas, 113–16
  vegetables grown in, 108–10
Creeping fig, *69*
Crocus, *136*
Cup of gold, *87*
Cutting gardens, 172–74

D

Daffodils, *43, 92*
Daylilies, *130, 138*
Deer, *23*
  rhododendrons avoided by, 54
  roses and, 53–54
Delphinium, *142*
Dill, *124*
Dogwood tree, *105*
Doty, Walter, 47, 67
Douglas, David, 108

Dwarf citrus, growth in
    small spaces, 154–55
Dwarf Valencia oranges, *155*

E

England
    cottage garden tradition in, 30–31,
      107–8
    gardening traditions, 29–31
    natural landscaping, 30
    rock gardens in, 31
English Flower Garden, The
    (Robinson), 30
English hedgerow, 22
English ivy, *51*
English Rock Garden, The (Farrer), 31
Essay on Modern Gardening, An
    (Walpole), 30
Eucalyptus, *139*

F

Farley, Walter, 49
Farrer, Reginald, 31
*Field Guide to the Birds of North
    America* (National Geographic
    Society), 78
Firethorn, hedges, *16–17*
Flowering dogwood tree, *105*
Flowers
    on vines, 70
    for woodland garden understory, 42
Fosberg, Ray, 140
Fountains, noise concealment and, 18
Foxglove, *93, 145*
Fragrance
    flowers for, 103–4
    honeysuckle, 78
    jasmine, 76–78
Fruit, growth in cottage gardens of, 113
Fuchsia, *102*

G

Gardening
    American traditions, 27
    appropriate, 129–39
    bog gardens, 39
    California tradition in, 36–39
    children's gardens, 174–76
    cottage gardens, 30–31, 38, 107–25
    cutting gardens, 172–74
    design and, 170–72
    English traditions, 29–31
    Japanese gardens, 38
    local plant adaptability, 96–98
    minimization of chores, 167–68
    naturalism in, 30
    number of people involved in, 12
    patience and, 54–55
    plant identification, 95–96
    plants for ease of maintenance, 90,
      100
    pleasure of, 9, 12–13
    rock gardens, 31
    Spanish tradition in, 32–36
    woodland gardens, 40–44
Gardening Illustrated, 30
Garden of Health, The, 124
Gartenmeister fuchsia, *102*
George W. Park Seed Company, 169
Giant snowdrop, *119*
Gold flame honeysuckle, *79, 81*
Goodman of Paris, 108
Gourds, *175*
Grape hyacinths, *30*
Grape vines, 75
Grasses
    in meadow gardens, 141–43
    ornamental, *130, 137*
    pampas, *140*
Ground cover, 55–60
Guide to the Birds (Peterson), 78

H

Halperin, Lawrence, 37
Heavenly bamboo, *163*
Hedges
    boxwood, *52*
    English hedgerow, 22
    fill in time for, 16–17
    peace and privacy and, 13–21
    plants for, 14–15
    tapestry hedge, 22
    trimming, 16
Hein, Herman, 131
Helleborus orientalus, *95*
Herbs
    in cottage gardens, 123–25
    growth in cities of, 150–54
Heriteau, Jacqueline, 95
Holly, *16, 101, 119*
Honeysuckle, *79, 81, 140*
    for fragrance, 78
Hooker, William Jackson, 108
Hops, 75
Hortus Sanitus, 124
Hostas, *92, 164*
House Beautiful, 37
House plants, cold-climate, 104
Hummingbird feeders, 23, 25
Hummingbirds, *144*

I

Iris, *114*
Ivy, *51, 56, 68*

J

Jackson and Perkins (rose dealers), 169
Japanese gardens, *38,* 38
    serenity within, 159–64
Japanese honeysuckle, *140*
Japanese maple tree, *61*
Japanese snowball, *162*
Jasmine, for fragrance, 76–78
Jekyll, Gertrude, 30, 108, 172

K

Keene, Carolyn, 49
Kenilworth ivy, *56*
Kent, William, 30
Kew Gardens (London), *28*
Kurt Bluemel, Inc., 143
K. Van Bourgondien and Sons, 169

L

Lady's eardrops, *102*
Lady fern, *44*
Landscape, redefinition of, 21–25
Landscaping, English natural, 30
Lawns
   American obsession with, 45–47
   banishment of, 9
   privacy and, 13
Lenten rose, *95*
Lettuce, *153*
Lilies, *57, 96, 104*
Lily-of-the-valley shrub, *103*
Lilypons Water Gardens, 169

M

Maccoby, Stirling, 95
McLaren, John, 70
Mandevilla splendens, 87
Manure, 115
Maple tree, 40–42, *98*
Marigold, *109*
Meadow gardens
   bloom succession in, 136–39
   establishment time for, 131–32
   evocative nature of, 144
   ornamental grasses in, 131, 141–43
   plants for, 132–36
   preparation for, 131
   regional plant behavior 139–41
   wildlife in, 143–44

Millay, Edna St. Vincent, *118*
Mint, *151*
Morning-glory, *71*
Morning-glory vine, *121*
Mount Hood daffodils, *92*
Mulching, 168

N

National Arboretum Book of
   Outstanding Garden Plants,
    The (Heriteau), 78, 95
Natural landscapes, 30

O

Onions, *153*
Orangeries, 154–55
Ornamental Gourds, *175*
Ornamental grasses, *130, 137*
  in meadow gardens, 141–43
Oxalis, 57

P

Paintbrush, *134*
Palm House (Kew Gardens), *28*
Palo Alto, tree-planting program in, 67
Pampas grass, *140*
Parsley, *154*
Passionflower, 74–75
Patios, 156–59
Peace, hedges and, 13–21
Peonies, *123*
Periwinkle, *51, 113*
Persimmon tree, *53*
Pesticides, 89–90

Peterson, Roger Tory, 78
Phillips (author), 100
Plant adaptability, 96–98
Plant identification, 95–96
Plant names, poetry of, 110–13
Plume poppies, *142*
Poetic garden, 110–13
Pools
   swimming, *37*
   waterlilies in, *20*
Poppies, *142*
Pots, dwarf citrus grown in, 154–55
Prairie gardens, 132
Privacy, hedges and, 13–21

Q

Queen Elizabeth rose, *82*

R

Raccoons, *23*
Red maple tree, *98*
Rhododendrons, *58, 61, 92, 93, 97, 99*
   deers' avoidance of, 54
Robinson, William, 30
Rock gardens, 31
Roses, *93, 95*
   Cécile Brunner, 60–62
   Climbing Blaze, *82*
   deer and, 53–54
   longevity of, 83–85
   Queen Elizabeth, *82*
   spectacular types, 83
Roses of Yesterday and Today, 169
Runner bean, 75, *153*

S

Sackville-West, Vita, 85, 140
Scarlet runner bean, 75, *153*
Secret Garden, The (Burnett), 49–50
Serenity, Japanese gardens, for, 159–64
Shade, plants for, 60
Shugakuin Imperial Garden (Japan),
      161
Silver lace vine, 70–72
Smith, Betty, 118
Smith and Hawkin (bulb distributors),
      169
Snapdragons, *120, 175*
Snowball, *162*
Snowdrop, *119*
Sound, foliage and fountains to absorb,
      18
Spain, gardening tradition in, 32–36
Spanish bluebells, *94*
Sprinkler systems, 54
Squirrels, *22*
Sulking, definition of, 62
Sunset New Western Garden Book,
      50, 95
Sunshine, 21
   plants for, 60
Sweet basil, *124, 151*
Sweet peas, *120*
Swimming pools, *37*

T

Tapestry hedge, 22
Tent caterpillars, 23–24
Terracotta pots, *158*
Terrariums, 29
Thompson and Morgan
      (seed company), 169
Town house gardens, 156–59
Tradescant, John (Elder and
      Younger), 97, 108
Tree Grows in Brooklyn, A (Smith), 118
Tree-of-heaven, *118*
Trees
   apple, *112*
   in cottage gardens, 116

flowering dogwood, *105*
garden designed around, 100–101
Japanese maple, *61*
persimmon, *53*
red maple, *98*
   as skeleton of garden, 100
tree-of-heaven, *118*
tulip, *98*
for urban areas, 118–19
weeping willow, *117*
woodland gardens, 40–44
Trees Around Us, The
      (Barber and Phillips), 100
Trumpet creeper, *69, 80*
Tulip tree, *98*

U

Urban wildlife, 22–23

V

Valencia oranges, *155*
Vegetables
   growth in cities of, 150–54
   growth in cottage gardens of, 108–10
Vines
   as appropriate in cities, 65–67
   to attract birds, 78–81
   for balconies, 72–74
   climate types, 87
   edible, 74–76
   effect on buildings, 67–70
   flowering, 70
   grape, 75
   hops, 75
   morning-glory, *121*
   passionflower, 74–75

scarlet runner bean, 75
silver lace, 70–72
to soften looks of walls, 67
wisteria, 72
See also Roses

W

Walpole, Horace, 30
Ward, Nathaniel, 29
Water
   for birds, *168*
   city supplies of, 129
   drip-trickle system for, 105, 168–69
   ground cover and, 58–60
   riparian rights and, 128
   for roses, 60–62
Waterlilies, *20*
W. Atlee Burpee Company, 169
Weeding, 169
Weeping willow tree, *117*
What Flower is That? (Maccoby), 95
White, Gilbert, 144
White Flower Farm, 169
Wilderness, landscape redefinition
      and, 22
Wildflower gardens, *129*
Wildflowers, *42,* 44–45
Wildlife, 22–23
   in meadow gardens, 143–44
Windbreaks, hedges as, 14
Window boxes, *150*
Winter aconite, *136*
Wisteria, *39,* 72, *73*
Woodland gardens, 40–44

Y

Yellow jacket wasps, 25